on track ...

Crowded House

every album, every song

Jon Magidsohn

SONICBOND

sonicbondpublishing.com

Sonicbond Publishing Limited
www.sonicbondpublishing.co.uk
Email: info@sonicbondpublishing.co.uk

First Published in the United Kingdom 2024
First Published in the United States 2024

British Library Cataloguing in Publication Data:
A Catalogue record for this book is available from the British Library

ISBN 978-1-78952-292-1

Typeset in ITC Garamond Std & ITC Avant Garde Gothic
Printed and bound in England

Graphic design and typesetting: Full Moon Media

on track ...

Crowded House

every album, every song

Jon Magidsohn

SONICBOND

sonicbondpublishing.com

Acknowledgements

I'm extremely grateful to Neil Finn for speaking with me in August 2023. His astonishment that someone was prepared to deconstruct every Crowded House recording and write about them was exceeded only by my own astonishment that Neil Finn would speak with me about those songs.

My sincere thanks to the Crowded House super-fans who read the nearly complete draft: Octavia Lamb, whose contagious love of the band prompted many additional questions to be answered, and Greg Vyrostko, whose musical insight provided invaluable detail (and corrections) to my naïve grasp of music theory.

As always, thanks to Deborah for her patience and support and for always singing along with 'passion and commitment.'

on track ...

Crowded House

Contents

Introduction

In the winter of 1986, aside from trying to get through high school unscathed, I was playing in a band. Most of the guys I knew growing up in Toronto played in bands, so I was nothing special, even though I thought I was. I'd cut my musical teeth on the arena rock mega-bands, such as Journey and Styx, a bit of prog and was into the 1980s ethos of U2, The Police and Joe Jackson. My band tried to express all of these influences, which, I now recognise, was near impossible considering our youthful naivete and barely tangible musical skills. Still, I believed in strong melodies and the power of a good hook.

Pete, my guitarist, walked into rehearsal one afternoon with an attitude of critical importance. 'Have you heard that song, 'Don't Dream It's Over'?' he asked. Of course, I'd heard it. It had been all over the radio and plastered on MuchMusic, Canada's music video station. 'It's going to be a monster hit. I'm telling you, Crowded House are going to be huge', he said. I liked Pete. He was a decent guitarist, if a bit heavy on the whammy bar, but I thought he was crazy. 'The song's alright,' I said. 'I just don't see it going anywhere.' I don't mind admitting I was wrong. But at the time, the melody didn't grab me, the lyrics made no sense to me and I thought that 'Hey now, hey now …' refrain was ridiculous.

The truth is that Neil Finn's song was more sophisticated than anything I expected to hear on my local top 40 radio station. His lyrics went over my head because they were not an ode to his favourite car or a declaration of love for his babe-du-jour. Rather, it was a poem about struggles against those that 'build a wall between us'. His voice, though warm and pleasant, didn't sound like anyone else's at the time. He wasn't rock 'n' roll raspy, melismatic or posing as someone other than who he was. The song's production seemed decent, but I'd never heard keyboards and guitars melding together to make 'that' sound before. I just didn't get it, so I wrote it off.

But the song hung around. When they released their next album, *Temple Of Low Men*, I was working in a popular downtown record shop and we had it spinning constantly. Suddenly, I was hooked on Crowded House. They were doing something different and that was the whole point. Neil Finn, Nick Seymour, Paul Hester and producer Mitchell Froom were crafting a new kind of pop song. They bent over backwards to inject as much musical originality, melodic integrity, original lyrics and sonic dynamism into the three-and-a-half-minute pop song as humanly possible. From what I could see, they were succeeding.

I connected to the music on an emotional level, which, as far as I was concerned, was the only legitimate way to connect with music. It didn't matter why it grabbed me, just that it grabbed me. *Temple Of Low Men* was one of the first CDs I'd bought – the technology was still in its infancy at this time – and I listened to it until I'd memorised every song. A few months later, I saw them in concert on their tour supporting that album. They became one of the artists whose every recording I had to have.

Pete was right about 'Don't Dream It's Over' – it became a hit all over the world. But did Crowded House become huge? I suppose it depends on who you ask. They were already popular in Australia and New Zealand. In Canada, they became one of those bands that we adopted as our own, particularly as they didn't gain the same sort of following in America, even less so in the UK. For many years, Crowded House made extra stops in Canada to satisfy that fan base and their singles were on regular rotation on the radio and MuchMusic. As Neil Finn shared with me during a Zoom call in August 2023:

> We spent more time in Toronto than just about any other North American city. *Temple Of Low Men* was quite a successful record there – I think 'Better Be Home Soon' was even a number-one song – whereas it didn't quite get there in America for reasons unknown.

One thing was clear: Neil Finn was a formidable songwriter, gathering praise from music fans and fellow musicians alike. At the time, his talent was only just usurped by his boyish charm and the youthful enthusiasm of his bandmates. It was the perfect recipe for success during the music video era, and despite many roadblocks and pitfalls along the way, he has managed to maintain the band to this day.

When Tim Finn was persuaded in 1977 to bring his little brother Neil into Split Enz as the second guitarist, he couldn't have known it would spark a creative explosion in his younger sibling. Tim's band had already been successful in New Zealand and Australia, touring the world in support of acts such as Roxy Music and Lou Reed. Their strong musicianship, united with jaunty melodies and a quirky stage persona, proved they were ready to be seen and heard. But Neil's participation brought them the one thing that had eluded them: a number one single called 'I Got You' (it was also in the top 20 in the UK and Canada).

Split Enz enjoyed another six or seven years of success with more hits, including 'Six Months In A Leaky Boat', 'One Step Ahead' and the very Crowded House-y 'Message To My Girl', written by Neil. Toward the end of this period, Tim left the band he created, leaving it in Neil's capable hands. The songs Neil Finn contributed to the later Split Enz releases showed him expanding his compositional explorations to include great musical hooks and unique melodic trajectories – the very tools that would help create Crowded House's identity.

By the time Split Enz played their last show in December 1984, Neil Finn and drummer Paul Hester – who had joined for their last album and tour – decided to form a new band. They met bassist Nick Seymour at the after-party of that final show and added guitarist Craig Hooper of the Australian band The Reels. They called themselves The Mullanes – after Finn's middle name – and, within months, had secured a record deal with Capitol Records.

Hooper didn't join them when they moved to Los Angeles to record what would become *Crowded House*, their first album, and the trio soon became the heart and soul of the new outfit. The name, chosen – over The Mullanes and Largest Living Things – by Capitol to reflect the conditions of the house they shared in the Hollywood Hills, suited the cheeky attitude of the three musicians and would ultimately play into the creation of their colourful stage performances. Everything was in place for the fuse to be ignited on a new musical adventure.

Now, more than 35 years after hearing them for the first time, I've tried to explore why it is they have continued to stay near the top of my musical pyramid. The main reason, as any fan would likely admit, is Neil Finn himself. His creativity, his sensitivity as a lyricist and, more than anything, his melodies have made him one of the most admired songwriters of his generation. Some of his melodies sit so perfectly within the chord structures and arrangements as to suggest there could be no alternatives. Finn's performances are direct and sincere.

However, Crowded House is not Neil alone. If it was, then Finn's solo albums and other collaborations would have been equally well-regarded. Though the band have evolved, it has always remained a collective effort.

What differs between Finn's output for Crowded House versus his other projects is largely down to the collaborative nature of the songs. What he created, originally with Nick Seymour and Paul Hester, was a unit that fashioned extremely friendly melodies and simple but imaginative arrangements and sounded like a band. Finn's solo work, alternatively, welcomed experimentation. Finn has found different outlets for him to explore his various musical paths. It's as if his marriage to Crowded House is kept fresh by his band, allowing him to go off and have a radical affair with himself.

What Neil Finn and his bandmates have been able to maintain for nearly 40 years and eight studio albums is a musicality seldom matched among their contemporaries, one that is both organic and heavily influenced by their Antipodean heritage. It is not just pop, rock, r&b, folk or worldbeat music – it is all of these things and more.

It's been a joy deconstructing each of these songs. As an older musician now, I wanted to understand what it is about Finn's talents as a songwriter and the band's musical spirit that keeps me interested. For me, it starts with melody. At the top of that musical pyramid are The Beatles. I'm a Paul guy, and within The Beatles, Paul was the king of melodies. In his decisive track-by-track book about The Beatles, *Revolution In The Head*, Ian MacDonald deconstructs the ways both Lennon and McCartney crafted their melodies:

> Lennon's melodies tend to move up and down as little as possible, weaving deviously through their harmonies in chains of repeated notes, two-note oscillations on minimal intervals or reiterated phrases ... McCartney's lines, by contrast, [range] freely across the stave in scalar steps and wide intervals,

often encompassing more than an octave … In other words, while the tunes of both are marked by an unusual incidence of non-chordal notes, McCartney's method is, in terms of intervals, 'vertical' (melodic, consonant), and Lennon's 'horizontal' (harmonic, dissonant).

Neil Finn, I dare say, is also a Paul guy. The majority of his melodies are unmistakably vertical, with few examples of a melodic line staying on one note for more than two or three syllables. He prefers to explore the full scale of whichever key he's singing in, playing around with notes that weave in and out of both major and minor chords in the same song. With the benefit of available demo recordings, it has also become clear that many of these songs have been the result of hard work and persistence. Crowded House make it seem easy.

Neil Finn told me via Zoom in 2023:

I wasn't being deliberate about it. But as time has gone on, the intricate nature of how melodies fit together has become endlessly fascinating to me. Sort of like secret codes for emotions, you don't know how to express in any other way ... I work on things to the level of obsession and my family look at me sometimes like I must be mad. And there is a certain madness attached to it. But I have had numerous occasions where something I've worked on for days, weeks and occasionally months suddenly clicks. I'll find one phrase or an extra little chord that supports it from being okay to being transcendent.

If I've been surprised by anything, it's the quality of Finn's lyrics. For an artist who has made his name as a melody maker, his ability to paint word pictures is equally impressive. He has cast himself as an anonymous Everyman with big feelings and his capacity for writing from unique perspectives on well-trodden themes is enormous. He is capable of exploring two contrasting perspectives in one song: the yin and yang, black and white, the joyous and the horrible. As a poet, he is at once concise and open to interpretation.

It is, then, a part of his craft how he melds lyrics and music in sometimes unpredictable ways. A song like 'A Sigh', from *Time On Earth*, for instance, is a balanced construction of music and lyric, perfectly expressing the resigned acceptance of the inevitable. Whereas 'Nobody Wants To', from the same album, uses one of Finn's most uplifting melodies as he sings about living in the emotional depths. Lyrics that show confusion, frustration or angst are decorated with rapturous melodies. Many of his songs tread this fine line of music matching words, proving that, in some cases, it doesn't matter – a sad song doesn't need to sound sad. Finn suggests through his music that our lives are complete only because of the extremes.

In the forthcoming chapters, I have tried to focus on the key elements of each song that make them interesting, including those songs that listeners may skip over. Even weaker songs yield interesting details. I've made note of the instances when Finn's vertical melodies are particularly worthy of mention. I've also included the rare moments when Finn's 'John side' pushed through.

Every so often, at least once per album, Finn touches base with his relationship with God to see how his faith is holding up during changing times. Having grown up with a devout Irish Catholic mother, he's never shied away from sharing the values he learned from her, as well as the questions he's inclined to raise due to his potentially claustrophobic Catholic upbringing. God appears in his songs as a character, as a framework for a lyric or sometimes just in passing. As Finn told Jeff Apter, author of *Together Alone: The Story Of The Finn Brothers*:

> It's a great fertile ground for pulling lyrics out … good rituals and imagery and lots of guilt. It's a very potent combination. I think you're blessed, really, to be brought up with some kind of weird dogma like that.

I had the great privilege of speaking directly with Neil Finn in August 2023. It was early morning in New Zealand – he admitted he was still wearing his pyjama bottoms – and was preparing for a full day recording vocals despite nursing a cold. Though I'd prepared questions for our discussion, the thrill of the conversation sent me off script. Nevertheless, Finn was generous with his time and considered responses, proving to me that he is a thoughtful artist who continues to evaluate his own progress, now well into his 60s. Throughout this book, I will refer to this interview as 'the 2023 Zoom conversation'.

Crowded House (1986)

Personnel
Neil Finn: guitar, piano, lead and backing vocals
Nick Seymour: bass
Paul Hester: drums, backing vocals
Additional musicians:
Mitchell Froom: keyboards
Tim Pierce: guitar
Jim Keltner: drums ('Now We're Getting Somewhere')
Jerry Scheff: bass ('Now We're Getting Somewhere')
Jorge Bermudez: percussion
Heart Attack Horns: horns
Noel Crombie: backing vocals
Jim Gilstrap: backing vocals
Andy Milton: backing vocals
Joe Satriani: backing vocals
Producer: Mitchell Froom ('Can't Carry On' produced by Eddie Rayner and Neil Finn)
Engineer: Tchad Blake, Dennis Kirk
Assistant Engineer: Steve Himelfarb
Mixer: Michael Frondelli
Recorded between November 1985 and March 1986 at Capitol Recording Studios (LA), Sunset Sound Factory (LA) and Platinum Studios (Melbourne)
Released in August 1986 on Capitol Records
Running time: 38:40
Highest chart position: UK: 99, US: 12, Australia: 1, Canada: 8
All songs by Neil Finn, unless otherwise specified

Neil Finn was 28 years old when *Crowded House* was released and was already a veteran on the international music scene for nearly ten years. Still, for someone relatively young, there's a maturity in the songwriting on this album. These are big songs with big themes, some quite dark: love, relationships, personal discovery, death, suicide, mental health.

However, Finn proved instantly that his lyrical content and poetic style could be balanced out by contagious melodies that arouse optimism and goodwill. The hooks on this album are instantly and forever memorable. Objectively, there isn't a weak song on this album, which produced no less than five charting singles.

This is a beautiful-sounding debut recording. Producer Mitchell Froom's input was as much musical as technical, resulting in a full sonic experience with tasty use of sounds outside of the normal three-piece rock band. It also included, as was popular at the time, participation from some of LA's most in-demand session musicians. They all helped to create a debut album that is sonically unified and musically diverse. In the context of Finn's career, it falls in that sweet spot between Split Enz's quirky pop and *Woodface*-era Crowded House.

In the 2023 Zoom conversation, Finn said:

> Mitchell was new to being a producer and I was with my new band, so we met each other at a good time. It was a convergence of thoughts. The band were in good shape. There were some difficult days making it, but overall, the band were becoming a band and learning how to operate together, but also having fun because we were good mates.
>
> It was an open book after Split Enz. The character of Paul's drumming and the new presence of Nick Seymour's bass playing – which was very different to our old bass player – meant that we knew we were capable of some different angles. Had we not been working with Mitchell – who had an American perspective, adding things like Hammonds and r&b bass lines – the album might have turned out to be very different, I think.

In the two years between the demise of Split Enz and the first Crowded House album, Finn had amassed a substantial collection of new songs, many of which he tried to bring to life with The Mullanes, the short-lived quartet that included Finn, Hester and Seymour, along with guitarist Craig Hooper. Teaming up with Froom not only cemented the creative team but provided the key to unlocking these unfinished songs, as Finn elaborated on during the 2023 Zoom conversation:

> It's always been the case that things are in a state of flux until you find that they just slot together all of a sudden by moving one beat, phrase or bar. It often puts things in the right place as if they've always been there, which is what you're always aiming for – to disguise the process as much as possible. Mitchell was, at the time, very big on making the song seem bolted together and encouraged me to knock bars out here and there to get into the next section sort of unexpectedly so that the listener keeps getting drawn forward into the song and it's less symmetrical.
>
> I became interested in it more than ever, discovering that you can really throw songs up in the air and examine them from every angle. I'm still deep in the middle of that process and, if anything, it's even more like that as time's gone on. It's like excavating an archaeological dig where you don't really know what you've got. It's like this endless jigsaw puzzle. It's a fascinating process. And then, in the end, once you paint over the top of it, it should sound like it was never broken in the first place.

'Mean To Me'

A new band opening their first album with a track about an obsessive fan is not an obvious choice, not least because few people would have heard of them at the time of this release, let alone be obsessed. However, like other songs on this album, Finn is quick to point out that he had a life before Crowded House. Indeed, the incident described in 'Mean To Me' refers to a rabid Split Enz follower.

Released as the first single, this lyric features a confusing use of pronouns. The first verse and chorus talk about this fanatical visitor in the third person: 'She came all the way from America'. From the second verse to the end, she's in the second person. 'So I talked to you for an hour.' This would prove to be a minor trend in Finn's songwriting.

What starts as a gentle-sounding song with just voice and acoustic guitar expands into a more soulful, densely arranged track with layered guitars, horns and a restless bass line. Finn's vocal performance borders on frantic at times, which meshes nicely with the circus-themed calliope that leads into the bridge.

Finn's natural use of vertical melodies is evident even from the start. In the opening four lines, he uses the first five notes of the major scale to great variety, with barely a note repeated unless used as a passing note. In the chorus, Finn sings an unpredictable major 6th interval on the word 'escape', literally breaking out of the melodic precedent he'd set for us. He even slides up to the note in a dramatic glissando as if to prove that his escape from this fan is even more treacherous than one might expect.

The final chorus opens some debate about who is down on their knees. Is it the groupie in a serviceable posture? Or is it the narrator begging her to leave him alone?

Also, for the first time, Finn's love of language is evident in the way he explores the word 'mean'. In the chorus, he expresses it in the context of connotation ('You know what it means to me') and also in the context of cruelty ('So please don't be mean to me'). By placing the two references so close together, he's also challenging the listener to navigate through the complicated morass of human relationships.

'World Where You Live'

The second track and second single from *Crowded House* is this story told by a man who sees his love slipping away. He seems to know that she's found someone stronger, steadier and more virile. However, being a man, he knows that all that glitters is not gold and that surely there is something else behind the façade of this Adonis. More than anything, he can't help wondering what she's thinking about when they're together: 'Do you climb into space, to the world where you live?'

The second verse suggests that he, too, might go off into another world when they're together. Maybe he has also found something more intriguing:

> And these four walls can never hold us
> We're looking for wide open spaces
> High above the kitchen

And we're strangers here
On our way to some other place

The verse melody uses that tried-and-true scheme of repetition with only slight variations on the first three lines. The fourth line pushes forward with a different melody that resolves on the tonic of the final chord.

Finn presents another one of his reliable songwriting tools by placing the verses in a minor key and the chorus in a major key. This, coupled with soaring harmonies and a bar of 2/4 leading into the chorus, helps show the contrast within one single thought.

'Now We're Getting Somewhere'

A perfect example of Finn seeing both sides of the picture: 'It never used to be that bad, but neither was it great. Somewhere in the middle, then'. In this instance, being in the middle, 'content and much too safe', is providing a feeling that the relationship is stagnant and in a constant state of stasis that, without interference, could turn into something altogether unwelcome, to put it mildly. The narrator feels he'll only be progressing – 'getting somewhere' – if she will 'lay me out with your heart ... push me back to the start', remembering the excitement of new love, never wanting to spend time apart.

The second verse says explicitly, 'I believe there is something wrong'. After another chorus, we are given a new 'two-sides' perspective when he admits, despite the pain in his heart, 'we can choose what we choose to believe'.

Again, Finn uses minor key verses to illustrate the problem and a major key chorus to reach for a solution. The whole song swings like a country ditty and Finn's passionate vocal performance is one of the strongest on this album. At 1:02, after the first chorus, there are two bars of arpeggiated guitar reminiscent of 'I'm A Believer' by The Monkees, which took its own inspiration from 'I Feel Fine' and 'Ticket To Ride' by The Beatles. It's a great moment of Crowded House paying homage to their musical forbears.

An accordion-like sound – played by Mitchell Froom on the keyboard – is used throughout, giving it the feel of a French romance. There is also great guitar work from session pro Tim Pierce. It's one of the songs recorded at a different LA session and includes guest luminaries Jerry Scheff, who played bass with everyone from Elvis Presley to Elvis Costello, and drummer Jim Keltner, who played with everyone else.

This was the third of five singles from this album and the only one not included on *Recurring Dream*, their first greatest hits package.

'Don't Dream It's Over'

As hope for a hit single faded after three previous failings, expectations for 'Don't Dream It's Over' were not high. Released finally as the fourth single from the debut album in the spring of 1987, it reached number one in New Zealand and Canada, number two in the US, number eight in Australia and it broke the top 30 in the UK. Not only did it turn the band's fortunes around, but to this day, the song remains Crowded House's most successful and most appreciated song.

Finn said in the 2023 Zoom conversation:

> It seemed to have an effect straight away. I wouldn't have had any idea it would become a big hit. We knew it was one of the best songs on the record, but it was hard to place ourselves in any context at that point because there weren't any bands around like us. That was the time of hair bands in the context of pop or rock music, and we didn't fit into that mould.
>
> It's always a mystery what connects with people. I immediately had a really deep feeling about it. I knew it was a pretty complete song. The words came together quite quickly, which is usually a good sign. Mitchell suggested the bass line for that, which gave it a certain feel that allowed it to be played on what at the time was called urban radio in America. It was a nice surprise that some of the black stations started playing that song.

Just like 'Now We're Getting Somewhere', this song starts with Finn seeing two sides of the same coin: 'There is freedom within, there is freedom without'. As if to emphasise the torrent of emotions this kind of double-think encourages, one may struggle to 'Try to catch the deluge in a paper cup'. It's too much to handle, even for the guy who's brave enough to attempt to put it into words. Still, though the struggles mount up, the singer stands stoic in the face of the battles and eases his companion's (or companions') own fears by offering, 'But you'll never see the end of the road while you're travelling with me'. It's his interpretation of the old saying, 'It'll be alright in the end. If it's not alright, it's not the end'.

Things are falling apart in the second verse ('Now I'm towing my car...'). He questions our desire to place value on our lives through the things we own. There are wars and other earth-threatening intrusions, but, the narrator asserts, you can rest easy because we're together. By the third verse, where once there were battles ahead, now there are only shadows of the struggles they endured.

Finn's famous chorus – 'Hey now, hey now…' – tries to put an end to the pinch-me-I'm-dreaming scenario. It's over. Nothing can hurt us now; we've gone through whatever was trying to pull us apart and though they try 'to build a wall between us, we know they won't win'. It's a multi-layered narrative smothered by a lush musical blanket.

Musically, this might sound like the most wistful song on the album, but lyrically, it is the most hopeful. Finn refers to the guitar riff as the Māori strum. 'It's the big backbeat 'cause you're playing drums as well as the guitar,' he told Kiwi music vlogger *The Sound*, referring to the percussive down-stroke over the strings on beats two and four. 'It's what I equate with really good sing-songs we've had growing up in New Zealand.' Auckland-based writer Daniel Taipua wrote in *The Guardian* in 2022:

> It is perhaps New Zealand's most distinctive and enduring musical sound, strummed on guitars across the country and often nicknamed jing-a-jik or rakuraku after the cadence it produces. It is a strum heard … at marae (meeting houses), family gatherings and competitive kapa haka (action dance) performances. At its most basic, the Māori strum uses three to four chords and a light upward strum matched with a heavy downward strum on the second and fourth beat to produce a rich combination of bass and treble, delivered with swinging percussion. The beauty of the strum, which has been fine-tuned at garage parties across the nation, is its simplicity and familiarity. Once you look for the strum, it shows up everywhere in New Zealand pop. Neil Finn credits it with forming the spine of a number of Crowded House songs.

In the 2023 Zoom conversation, Finn said:

> There's a half a bar missing before the organ solo starts, which is the bane of my life because whenever I'm teaching it to someone, I have to tell them, 'Hang on, there's a half bar missing there'. But it does move the song forward.

Mitchell Froom's organ solo and Nick Seymour's bass line have contributed to 'Don't Dream It's Over's iconic existence and inclusion as one of 80s pop music's timeless treasures. Stevie Nicks, when introducing this song during Finn's brief participation in Fleetwood Mac 30 years later, called it one of the greatest melodies ever written.

Finn told Zane Lowe of Apple Music in 2021:

> It's had a really great life. I enjoy the mystery and magic of it. It's had a couple of Te Reo versions in New Zealand, which is a really pleasurable thing to hear. There's an aboriginal version of it and it's been translated into so many other languages. It's fantastic.

'Love You 'Til The Day I Die'

Counted in with a shrieking, demonic (and inarticulate) '1, 2, 3, 4' as if the singer is constantly in monster mode, this is the Jekyll and Hyde story: 'There's closets in my head where dirty things are kept, that never see the light of day'.

'I believe in doing things backwards', he sings in the chorus, either by choice or by necessity. The narrator assumes that if he can convince the one he loves that, even in his Mr Hyde state, he can be loved in return, then surely he can be loved at any moment.

The bridge lyric paints a picture of the typical horror film motif. Dr Jekyll is in his laboratory mixing up his concoctions and hoping to hide his dark side: 'Frost on the windowpane, the sound of pouring rain, all makes me glad of you'. To emphasise the backward approach, he screams (to himself, perhaps), 'Know the answer before you know the question'. Then, in one of Finn's edgiest vocal performances, he desperately cries, 'I'm alone. Always alone'.

The melody's opening lines use minor second intervals over a B major chord to strike an ominous, haunted tone. The chorus has a tight chord progression with guitar and horn stabs playing thirds on the third beat of every bar to give it a sense of restricted movement as if our singer is caged. Every musician is playing hard and Finn's vocals belie the warm precedent he sets in 'Don't Dream It's Over'. According to Finn (neilfinn.com): 'This one started as a little mandolin ballad and ended up as the heaviest song on the first album.'

'Something So Strong' (Neil Finn/Mitchell Froom)
During the 2023 Zoom conversation, Finn said:

> 'Something So Strong' was originally quite a pretty ballad on acoustic guitar. And he [Froom] suggested putting an r&b bassline on it, making it more up-tempo. I think to this day, he thinks he might have made a mistake about that. However, it was a hit, so we'll give him some credit for that.

The fifth and final single from this album, 'Something So Strong' is the most straightforward love song on this album. But, typically for Finn, it's seen from the other side. Finn never denies how wonderful love can be but is exploring the other possibilities brought on by its power. He never claims love *will* make you weep or love *will* leave you cold, he only suggests that it *can* do these things. Something as strong as love has the potential for great joy but also for great treachery: 'Something so strong could carry us away'. To where, we might wonder?

Despite his glass-half-empty perspective, Finn suggests that the dreadful, distressing elements of love might also be what makes it so exciting. Love 'can make you run for cover, roots that spread so deep bring life to frozen ground' and 'a taste of jealousy is like a lust for gold'. As long as you're getting the same rush, he says, what does it matter how miserable you are? Yet, the melody and groove move along in a bouncy, country lilt that will have people line dancing in the aisles.

In the bridge, the narrator suggests that recognising love's shortcomings or, perhaps, even falling out of love will help keep you feeling younger:

> I've been feeling so much older
> Frame me and hang me on a wall
> I've seen you fall into the same trap
> This thing is happening to us all.

This has a simple arrangement that spotlights the lyric. The opening guitar has a full sound (certainly double-tracked, at least) and Froom's organ is a welcome colour to this. With a song this complete (intro, verse, chorus, verse, chorus, bridge, guitar solo, double chorus, outro), it can be surprising to learn that it's less than three minutes long. Finn commented on this in the 2023 Zoom conversation:

> I've probably always been interested in and satisfied with the three-minute format in pop songs. I enjoy it. I'm now much less concerned with whether I'm listening to pop music, African music or Indian music and how long it is. But in those days particularly, I focused on some of the great pop music that I admired, and I was quite happy to work in that structure. We were trimming stuff down. Mitchell and I were interested in the idea that the song would keep moving forward.

'Hole In The River' (Neil Finn/Eddie Rayner)
There's little mystery to the story of this lyric. Even in concert, Finn would introduce this song as factual, relating the story of his auntie's suicide by drowning. As Finn told the *New Zealand Herald* in 2001:

> I would hope it has become what, at the time, I thought it was: the most positive way I could reflect on something which was tragic. I like the feeling when songs inhabit spaces that are difficult for people to talk about, so they gain some degree of empathy or comfort from listening to them.

Ever searching for that perfect melodic hook, Finn found a way to make this song worthy of an earworm despite there being no chorus. The melody of the opening line sets the right mood with its use of the Aeolian scale. Rather than a straight minor scale, he uses the flattened seventh (flat7) on the word 'hole', which is at once foreboding and comforting. The memorable bridge is in an unusual position between the first and second verses: 'I hope she was dreaming of glory, miles above the mountains and plains, free at last'.

He brings in a new character, 'my father', in the second verse, adding another level of tragedy to the story: 'She was coming to see him, but something changed her mind'. In a collection of songs that show a preoccupation with sorrow, emotional struggles and death, this is the most chilling line on the whole album. Finn can only imagine the state of mind of someone so desperate to die, she changes her plans in order to carry it out. There's a lovely bit of poetry where 'a cold wind' becomes 'the sound of desperate breathing'.

The haunting arrangement includes percussive rhythm guitar and heavily reverbed guitar overdubs. In lieu of a chorus is the simple refrain, 'there is no return', which is followed by an instrumental interlude coming across, inexplicably, as a combination of saloon piano and the Hallowe'en Party soundtrack. Listening to the original Split Enz demo from 1984, Paul Hester's 'I'm Still Emotional' rap seems to justify the intensity of this section, albeit detracting from the overall emotional integrity of the song. A false ending begins at 3:02 as the skeletal keyboards quickly fade, dancing into the moonlight before leaping back in for a proper fadeout that echoes the earlier interlude, complete with menacing horn stabs and ghostly voices.

'Can't Carry On'

This appears to be a song about a serial one-night-stander. The feeling of the singer being adored is palpable, but so is the sense of clear dissatisfaction and shame of acting on it: 'Why do I kid myself ... It's four in the morning should know better/But she can weave a spell ... Making me feel like somebody special'.

The song opens with a mysterious sound that takes over from the haunting outro of 'Hole In The River' before plunging straight into the main groove: a solid four-on-the-floor rock beat that never relents. The verses, in particular, are full of some very satisfying guitar fills.

The rousing chorus bursts through the gloom and spells it out as Finn sings in an appealing falsetto: 'Can't carry on this way (just go to sleep)'. But despite all of his efforts to convince himself to stop, he admits: 'Well, here we go again'. In the second verse, it seems he's looking for the strength to stop this behaviour, but he can't just buy it at the shop: 'Though I look everywhere I never seem to find it ... drown it in alcohol'. The silver lining is that the events are 'hard to remember in the morning'.

The third verse continues this exploration, with the narrator admitting that, due to his loneliness, he might just benefit from trying to get to know these women: 'Tell you about myself if you're in the mood to listen ... This is a lonely world'. But even that backfires: 'When you get what you wanted you want to leave'.

The bridge – a self-chastising 'honestly I want to free myself from the burden of inaction' – uses the chorus chords in A major, then modulates (changes key) up to B major – with help from a huge guitar slide (glissando) high in the mix – for the final chorus. The result is that the song starts in B minor and ends in B major despite using a modulation.

'I Walk Away'

An adopted Split Enz song (originally released on their 1984 album *See Ya 'Round*) about the pending demise of the band, it's reworked here as a fairly standard break-up song that, in Finn's hands, turns into a story of two sides in which the blame is equally attributed.

The first notable element is the guitar intro, which has the unmistakable sound and feel of Bryan Adams' 'Summer Of '69', released two years earlier – it's even in the same key. In contrast with the Split Enz version that plods headlong through the song, the Crowded House version is more varied and strategic in terms of dynamics and instrumentation.

This narrator goes on an emotional journey as he dissects the end of a relationship. Verse one starts with a beautiful, biblical reflection: 'You came out of this world to me, my life parted like the Red Sea'. The wonder of a love that 'ended in confusion' has him wondering why. The chorus states plainly, 'It's hard to let go of all that we know, as I walk away from you'. In verse two, the confusion has evolved into anger: 'Black words slipping off my tongue. I say forget it – it's over'. He is not having a good day and now admits, 'The sun always sets with room for regrets, as I walk away from you'. Yet, by the final chorus, the narrator, perhaps secretly, is wondering if they might give it one more try. He still can't shake the memory of all the good things they shared: 'Give it to me, your inspiration. Give to receive, find all we need'. But still, 'I walk away'.

After a brief instrumental interlude starting at 1:56 – that includes some fine interplay among the musicians – there's a half verse where he finally reveals what he thinks pushed them apart: 'Just a slave to ambition. Tension your permanent condition. So much you've always wanted'. Or maybe, once again, he's singing about himself: 'Too much given you a sore head'.

'Tombstone'

More imagery of a troubled religious past greets us here, this time wrapped up in a Wild West theme. From the terrific opening line – 'Look at all the plans I made, falling down like scraps of paper' – the narrator can see the memories of the life he'd thought was promised to him cascading around him like fallout. Until 'from the past a rumour comes' and he decides to take one of those scraps of paper and 'throw the memory in an open fire' so that, once again, he can be free from the pain of what might have been.

The second verse suggests that we are all a work in progress, ever moving forward toward some kind of peace. You can't go back, nor can you deny that your wheels have already covered that bit of track behind you: 'Beware the passenger, the train already left the station. We are neither home nor at work, we are moving'.

The Wild West motif comes to its peak in the second chorus: 'Roll back the tombstone 'til the Lone Ranger rides again ... Ride across the open plain'. In this ambiguous reference, the narrator could be the Lone Ranger or might simply be someone watching this unfold from afar.

With the song framed around the acoustic guitar, this could be a kind of campfire song and there is some nice interplay between guitars. However, this is one song that could have benefitted from less production. There is some overuse of keyboard pads, particularly in the verses, and a guitar solo that sounds more like *James Bond* than *The Lone Ranger*.

'That's What I Call Love' (Paul Hester/Neil Finn)

Musically and melodically the least interesting song on *Crowded House*, this seems a strange way to end the album. Still, it shouldn't be surprising that this is not your typical love song. The lyric has all the fingerprints of Hester's wild imagination but includes Finn's penchant for a contrary approach. If it wasn't for all the pain, desperation, hopelessness and moments of feeling like the life was being sucked out of you, it just wouldn't be love at all. Verse two stretches out longer with some quick-fire reflections on this intoxicating misery: 'Show me the door, I'm abandoned here. You swim, I sink … you bend I break. I die tonight'.

Live performances have shined a brighter light on 'That's What I Call Love'. The funky rhythm section groove is matched by Finn's Nile Rodgers-style guitar comping, giving it a positively 'Le Freak' buoyancy that is missed on the album version. They have also, on occasion, altered the chorus lyric to include 'brothers kissing brothers … sisters kissing sisters. That's what I call love'. Make of that what you will.

Temple Of Low Men (1988)

Personnel
Neil Finn: guitar, lead and backing vocals
Nick Seymour: bass, backing vocals
Paul Hester: drums, backing vocals
Additional musicians:
Tim Finn: backing vocals
Mitchell Froom: keyboards
Richard Thompson: guitar on 'Sister Madly'
Alex Acuña: percussion
Heart Attack Horns: horns
Producer: Mitchell Froom
Engineer: Tchad Blake
Mixer: Bob Clearmountain
Recorded between 1987 and 1988 at Platinum Studio (Melbourne) and Sunset Sound Factory (LA)
Released in July 1988 on Capitol Records
Running time: 38:04
Highest chart position UK: 99, US: 40, Australia: 1, Canada: 10
All songs by Neil Finn

Any notion that Crowded House were going to capitalise on the success of their debut by putting out another album of guitar-based, three-minute pop songs should have been put safely to bed within hearing the first few seconds of the opening track. The dominance of keyboards, the Motown bass lines featured high in the mix, the more thoughtful lyrics and an overall slower tempo help to make *Temple Of Low Men* an even more sophisticated album than its pop-trio predecessor.

Froom's production is quieter and more sparse, which allows for the individual musical performances to shine through. If there had been any risk of falling victim to the second album jinx – when a successful debut album is difficult to follow up because it's often recorded hastily and under pressure – Finn didn't see it that way, as he said in the 2023 Zoom conversation:

> The second album was actually very enjoyable to make; it was easier and quicker than the first album. We had done a lot of touring at that point and actually going out to promote that record was more difficult. We had gotten fatigued about certain aspects of ourselves; maybe we weren't on form. But the recording of it was fine. The album didn't do as well in America, but we were still capable of putting on a pretty good show. The album had some darker themes and it got talked about as having downbeat lyrics. I didn't think it was.
>
> I did get a letter some years later from someone who was a promotions guy at Capitol apologising to me for dropping the ball on the second

Crowded House record, which I wasn't even aware of. But those things just pass by.

The extensive touring for *Temple Of Low Men* continued at an exhaustive pace. In an attempt to counter the fatigue, the band simplified some live appearances, preferring to perform acoustically. These performances highlighted their musicianship alongside the lively personalities that had become so obvious in their early music videos. Finn elaborated in the 2023 Zoom conversation:

> We were enjoying each other's company and on stage particularly. We were quite a buoyant band and we injected a lot of joy and energy into the room, especially while playing acoustic shows soon after the album came out. We started doing these three-piece busking shows and that's when we really became a band and learned how to sing together, particularly with Paul Hester in there and the banter between us, which drew people in. It was an unusually intimate performance style that people really responded to. It was unplugged before the phrase was coined, I suppose.

Former Split Enz bandmate Eddie Raynor joined Crowded House on tour as their keyboard player, replaced midway by Mark Hart, who would eventually join full-time.

The album's title was pulled from a book of euphemisms that engineer Tchad Blake brought into the studio for entertainment purposes, as Finn told DJ Jeremy Ansell in 2016 for the Deluxe Edition booklet:

> We were just being facetious, really. But it also sounded weighty, like it had some kind of mystical significance. 'In The Lowlands' was in the same book.

Crowded House released another five singles from *Temple Of Low Men*, with 'Better Be Home Soon' reaching the top ten worldwide.

'I Feel Possessed'

Froom's ominous minor 2nd keyboard motif sets the mood for the album in the opening few bars of 'I Feel Possessed', another perfect example of Finn's unique perspective in a love song. Obsession isn't nearly strong enough to evoke the connection this narrator feels with his lover, so he's taken it to a paranormal extreme: 'I could feel you underneath my skin, as the wind rushed in sent the kitchen table crashing'. This is love to an *Exorcist* degree.

Realistically, there are two interpretations, but they appear to be two sides of the same coin: first – our singer is in love, 'possessed' if you will, by a woman who is herself literally possessed in a Satanic kind of way. Second – she is the devil incarnate and her love actually possesses him, much to her denial: 'She says I could never do that' opens the song.

Verse two contains perhaps the quintessential Neil Finn lyric: 'It was one of those times wished I had a camera on me'. It's a line that is both specific in detail and broad enough in context to lead the lyric anywhere. When we finally learn what he's looking at and why he might want to capture this moment, it's not what we expect: 'Six foot off the ground, well, I know how that sounds'. Again, whose possession is he referring to? Is he six feet above the earth, or is she? To him, it hardly seems to matter: 'I just want to be there when it happens again'.

The undeniable humour in this scenario – a playful humour that has always sprung forth from the trio in their interviews and videos – is again cleverly disguised by a hypnotic minor-key verse melody – reminiscent of 'Love You 'Til The Day I Die' from the first album – only to burst open into a rousing major-key melody in the chorus.

Finn's guitar starts to sneak in halfway through the first verse but never rises to play the commanding role it did on most of the earlier songs. Even in the coda, which vamps on two simple chord changes, the organ leads the way.

Finn quotes two songs from the 1960s: 'People Are Strange' (The Doors, 1967) and 'God Only Knows' (The Beach Boys, 1966) – both, in their own way, are about a possession of sorts.

'Kill Eye'

Arguably, Finn invented the concept of cancel culture before the social media generation put a name to it. In the context of this song, the light is shining on the television, which, at the time, was arguably the only media that mattered. American televangelist Jimmy Swaggart made his tearful confession about sexual impropriety, begging the lord – and his own flock – for forgiveness. It made for compelling TV, but moreover, it made Swaggart disappear. He could no longer continue preaching over the airwaves and certainly lost millions of holy dollars in the process. As America watched with fascination and – to some, perhaps – a fair amount of Schadenfreude, screens glowing like the devil's glare – the kill eye – everyone knew what this public confession would result in for its subject: utter cancellation. It's Swaggart's whispering plea that begins the track: 'I beg you, forgive me'. The irony couldn't have been lost on those who watched, seeing this man who claimed religious immunity wandering 'halfway to hell and beyond' and begging to be swallowed up by the earth for his transgressions. He is dying under the gaze of those who love him and those who hate him.

By far the heaviest song on *Temple Of Low Men*, 'Kill Eye' is at once funky and a 'Helter Skelter' reboot. Finn uses his screaming McCartney voice in this vocal performance to great effect: 'I want the earth to open up'. The insertion of musical transition figures played in unison between guitar, bass and keyboard provides a punishing – but still intensely musical – mood to the arrangement. This is all very listenable for a song without an obvious chorus.

'Into Temptation'

This song is 'Kill Eye's opposite. If Finn was fascinated by the spectacle of watching a man fall from grace, he was also just as fascinated with that feeling of falling. Whether or not the narrator of this song actually succumbs to his temptation or merely suffers from the act of being tempted, all Finn wants us to know is that there was 'an open invitation for me to go into temptation, knowing full well the earth will rebel'. 'The earth', in this case, is this man's world – the life he knows and accepts as his own. Temptation that takes away his breath and weaves a kind of spell is enough to cradle him 'safe in the wide open arms of hell'. It's a sensation that comforts and tortures in equal parts.

The bridge offers a romantic image of descending into hell: 'We can go sailing in. Climb down'. These words rise out of his body in an ecstatic, falsetto climax over strong major chords. This sweet-sounding ballad-like moment is brought to a dynamic summit by orchestral strings.

The final lyric – 'Don't tell' – serves a dual purpose: a warning to the siren who has tempted him and a warning to himself as he lies sleepless 'in the last slow hours of morning' as if temptation should always remain a secret, regardless of any result from it.

According to Australian media outlet *Junkee*:

> If you ever needed an example of how convincing Neil Finn's songwriting is, consider this: Sharon Finn thought Neil was cheating on him because of this song.

By way of a response, Finn told Australian radio in 1988:

> I'm from a fairly conservative, middle-class, Catholic background, so, for me, I can't separate sex from the guilt and faithfulness and all that. So, it's written not about myself but about a state of mind that I'm familiar with.

The band pull off the neat trick of orchestrating a nearly constantly ascending bass line while singing about descending into hell. Though the song is firmly rooted in E minor, there is enough chordal movement to reflect the narrator's unsettled feelings. Hester's brushes on the snare drum create an abrasive contradiction to the gentle language of the lyric and deepen the minor-key mood. As Nick Seymour told Radio New Zealand's Jeremy Ansell for the 2016 Deluxe Edition:

> There's a beautiful temperature in the touch of that rhythm section between Paul and me. The bass drum is just so gingerly touched. We gradually devolved that ability to, I think, emote.

'Into Temptation' was the third single issued from this album.

'Mansion In The Slums'

As many songwriters have done before, this is Finn's take on the cost of fame, the struggle to cope with success and money and the all-too-common scenario of a manager taking advantage. Though it's unlikely to be completely autobiographical, Finn waits until late in the song to be explicit: 'What I mean is, would you mind if I had it all?' Why not have it all when – as he screams through the coda and at the final chord – 'It'll soon be over'. Even an artist with a lengthy career assumes their success won't last forever. That's why professional athletes justify their eye-watering salaries, why musicians like Billy Joel and Alanis Morissette sue their managers and why poets like Finn use their voice and platform to publicly explore the desire to have it all.

Included are the other common tropes of fame: Andy Warhol's noted quote on the topic ('The taste of success only lasts a half an hour or less'); New Age trends ('an isolation tank') often explored by the famous; and the existential threat of losing it all when the next young thing comes along ('With somebody else always breathing down your neck').

With all of this subtext, however, according to the band, it's a rather comical song, as they told Jeremy Ansell for the 2016 Deluxe Edition:

> Finn: It's basically about LA. It's a tongue-in-cheek song, it's not supposed to be taken too seriously, but it deals with a few of the conflicting …
>
> Seymour: Paradoxes …
>
> Finn: … of having success and living in a town like Los Angeles, which revolves around ratings.

When the narrator states, 'Sometimes I get it free', he lets out an uncomfortable, embarrassed chuckle. Here's a figure who's achieved success, the likes of which most people can only dream about, and has the option to live in a mansion in the hills above Los Angeles, yet people give him gifts and offer him tables at restaurants.

An elaborate arrangement includes keyboard and horn fills peppering the song. At 2:06, during Mitchell Froom's piano solo, you might spot the horns quoting the melody of the keyboard introduction to 'World Where You Live'.

'When You Come'

Released as a single in Australia only, this is one of the most satisfying songs on *Temple Of Low Men*. The sexual implications in the lyric are obvious, but Finn looks deeper as if the mere suggestion of meeting up is foreplay. Finn imagines that the act of these lovers meeting up is on a gladiatorial scale, where danger lurks along every stage of the journey. 'When you come across the sea, me like a beacon guiding you to safety', he begins. And the imagery only gets more spectacular from there: 'And when you come the hills will breathe like a baby pulled up heaving from the bottom of the ocean.' These earth-shattering moments are described by Finn using his raspier, more urgent-sounding voice. Finally, when he sees her, he opines: 'I'll know you by the thunderclap pouring like a rain of blood to my emotions'. His emotions, he unselfconsciously admits, are mythological in scale.

There is a lovely adherence to the tightly written lyric in this song. The music accommodates for however long is needed to sing the lines through irregular phrase lengths. Starting in E major (but with the melody beginning on the fourth of the chord, it nearly sounds minor), sometimes they wait three bars before moving to the next chord, sometimes four or five bars.

The chorus, however, leaves us with a question: 'And that is why I stumble to my knees ... I know I could never let you down'. Does he have faith that, regardless of his actions, he will always satisfy her needs? Or is he suggesting that he would never allow his actions to let her down? Or both?

At 3:17, after a short instrumental break – where Finn's guitar is played like a mandolin – there is a slight shift in the groove, thanks mainly to Hester's semiquaver rolls on the snare. There is an immediate sense that this section will build in intensity, which it does, as Finn sings about the feeling of seeing her rising from the sea 'like a slow volcano, burning and exploding' until finally erupting to 'cover the ground with ashes'. There are few examples of musical orgasms in popular music, but this is certainly one of the strongest ones. It's a climactic ending section that draws the song out to be the longest track on the album at 4:45. Too long for top 40 radio, but it's a great way to wrap up side one of the original album. As the band told Jeremy Ansell for the 2016 Deluxe Edition:

> Finn: I still maintain that it was about the second coming of the Messiah and the birth of the universe. It was about stars exploding in space and stuff. People are going to have filthy minds and think I'm talking about orgasms, but that's bullshit.

Still, he admits there are the inescapable 'sexual overtones here and there but nothing too serious'.

As Finn sings into the chorus, 'And why…', it's another use of the major sixth interval (see 'Mean To Me'). This interval is wide enough to use dramatically, but because it's not the fifth, which is a naturally resolving interval, or the seventh, which wants to resolve up to the octave, the sixth wants to take us somewhere unpredictable. It continues the narrative.

'Never Be The Same'

Neil Finn has never been able to state clearly what this song is about. But from the outside, it sounds like a song about domestic abuse: 'You slip with the back of your hand, you're taking it out on the one you love. I couldn't believe it'. People have witnessed it but did nothing to stop it. There is only the passing acknowledgement that all those involved will 'never be the same'. In the second verse, Finn uses his powers of varied perspectives to create a cryptic speaker. Is it the abused or the abuser? 'How long must I wait for you to release me? I pay for each mistake while you suffer in silence'.

However, the wonderfully optimistic chorus posits that 'we might still survive'. With the repetition of 'never be the same', he might also be suggesting that they could live a different life without the same daily antagonism.

More than any other song in this album, 'Never Be The Same' sounds as if it could have been on the first album. It harkens back to the sound of the trio – guitar, bass, drums and vocals – with a sparing use of keyboards. Only during the breakdown at 2:48 – 'And every time I hear you' – does the keyboard accordion come to the fore, but is then buried again during the coda.

'Love This Life'

Knowing what we know about the history of the band, specifically drummer Paul Hester's struggle with depression and ultimate suicide, this song appears particularly prescient. Maybe Finn was reaching out to his friend in 1988 in the hope that Hester would remember that he is loved and that, even against 'a million to one odds', there are countless things for him to love about life.

An intoxicating arpeggiated guitar line starts the song and binds the arrangement of mid-tempo pop with lush vocals. For such a musically smooth sound, Seymour's bass is surprisingly busy. But his prancing line helps drive the song forward, stopping it from getting bogged down by the tight lyric.

Finn, again, uses E minor to outline the character's inner turmoil before elegantly switching to E major whenever he sings 'Love this life'. It's a perfect marriage of music and lyrics to drive the narrative of this song. The lower octave lead vocal doubling on 'seal my fate', 'no one is wise' and 'whatever you've done' lends an even more ominous tone to the devilish possession this character might be feeling. The second verse is cleverly truncated, starting at what would be the second melody line: 'And so they threw you in jail'. The instrumental bridge, starting at 2:17, has a 'Hole In The River' creepiness to it as if connecting the two songs about days 'when you'll never have to feel no pain'.

This song is another indicator that Crowded House are a band of opposites. They present themselves as jokers and jesters, prancing around with big goofy smiles in their videos while playing songs about weighty subjects – and they get away with it.

'Sister Madly'

More references to a dark mind, wrapped up in a jaunty, vaudevillian swing tune, crop up here. Interpretations aside, there is a grimness to this lyric that contributes to the notion of Neil Finn as a deeply thoughtful lyricist. He gave his own interpretation to Jeremy Ansell for the 2016 Deluxe Edition:

> I think it's about me, really, and my mad scramble for success and acknowledgement. 'All the people that you're standing on' and all that. The verses, to me, describe an earnest little man running around in a fit, trying to find the land of his dreams, being in magazines and stuff. Then the chorus is just like a recurrent nightmare from childhood, waking up and my sister screaming after having a nightmare.

How do the two ideas link, one might wonder?

Richard Thompson, whom producer Froom was about to start working with for his next album *Amnesia*, was brought in to perform the guitar solo. Thompson ended up touring with Crowded House on more than one tour, doing an opening, solo acoustic set and coming on to share the stage on 'Sister Madly'.

Despite the presence of guitar royalty, it's the rhythm section that is particularly noteworthy on this recording. Hester's brushwork is stellar. Some of his fills are so imaginative that it can be tricky to follow where beat one is. He has created the perfect groove alongside Seymour's impressive walking bass line. All in all, the band create the perfect stylistic pastiche that makes this song both lost in time and also timeless.

'In The Lowlands'

This is a beautifully written lesson on geography and loneliness. Here, Finn takes his metaphorical command of poetry to the ultimate degree by not once breaking from the character of a man lost in unkind terrain. But it's not only about being lost. It's also very much about one person's struggle to connect with another person and, in the process of working toward that connection, encountering myriad obstacles.

Finn gets more points for another superb opening lyric: 'Oh Hell, trouble is coming out here in panic and alarm'. 'Oh Hell…' not only raises the trouble factor but also makes it personal. We see the ominous storm brewing through his eyes, all because of two little words.

He ends the first chorus with another line that comes from the gut of the troubled wanderer. As 'fear will take the place of desire' in this scenario, it would be understandable if he just gave up. Maybe Finn is singing about getting lost in actual terrestrial lowlands. Or maybe he's just feeling low. Or he could be trying to push the euphemism to its ultimate extent. We don't know exactly who or what he's looking for but we're along for the ride as he intones desperately: 'Try for Heaven's sake'. It is an aching and piteous cry for help.

Again, Finn gets the relationship between major and minor spot on. He sings forlornly and stays in the C# minor throughout the verses. The chorus starts on the E major chord, the minor third of the tonic, but when he sings 'lowlands', it's over a C#sus4 chord that absolutely brings the chorus alive. In this example, the major chord doesn't necessarily lighten the mood (like in

'Love This Life', for example) but heightens the sense of alarm experienced by the protagonist. The arrangement is dominated by bottom-heavy drums, walking bass and simple interplay between guitar and organ. The instruments leave ample space for vocals and harmonies, all leading up to an instrumental coda that allows the band to riff out on some of their well-honed 'lost-in-the-lowland' darkness.

'Better Be Home Soon'

Musically and structurally, this is one of the most traditional pop songs in the Crowded House discography and is the least representative of *Temple Of Low Men*. The chorus only uses a few simple chords: C major, F major and G major. It's no wonder that this song can get an audience singing. Objectively, it's a country and western song (and has been covered by more than one country musician). For a band that can create unique landscapes with their music, it's refreshing to know that they are also capable of simplifying to great success, even on a song placed at the end of an album.

Finn has also said that this is written from a woman's point of view: both the lyric 'When you get back home maybe I'll be gone' and the song's title suggest she is tired of waiting for her man to bring her what she needs. However, from the male perspective, 'I know I'm right for the first time in my life' could easily follow the generalised trope of the woman always being right in a relationship while the man acquiesces.

But Finn does his usual best at seeing both sides of this domestic scene. Even though the narrator is clearly feeling the burden of 'lies and deception' and admits to being able to 'start again, you can depend on it', they still want their partner to come home. This more universal lyrical theme, aside from the sing-along chorus, could be why this was chosen as the first single and connects with so many listeners.

Finn told Zane Lowe of Apple Music in 2021:

> I'm quite happy to have songs that are open-ended enough to lend themselves to any occasion, and that song has indeed been embraced by people who've been homesick, embraced by people who've separated from their loved ones, embraced by people who've just fallen in love.

Froom's organ solo has become iconic since its recording, a neat trick for a band that, at this point, didn't have an official keyboard player. After his solo – just as, out of nowhere, the band introduce two new chords, Fsus2 and Bb9, toward the final verse – Finn can be faintly heard singing something. Later live recordings suggest that he's singing: 'When the lights go down, when you've had your fill, when there's nothing left'.

Woodface (1991)

Personnel
Neil Finn: guitar, keyboards, lead and backing vocals
Tim Finn: piano, guitar, lead and backing vocals
Nick Seymour: bass, backing vocals
Paul Hester: drums, percussion, keyboards, lead and backing vocals
Additional musicians:
Mitchell Froom: keyboards
Ricki Fataar: drums, percussion ('All I Ask', 'There Goes God', 'Weather With You')
Chris Wilson: harmonica
Peter Bucknell: violin
Vince Parsonage: viola
Alex Acuña: percussion
Geoffrey Hales: percussion
Jack Mack: brass
David Hidalgo: accordion
Jorge Callendrelli: string arrangement, conductor
Sharon Finn: backing vocals
Mark Hart: keyboards
Stuart Ellison: keyboards
Producer: Mitchell Froom, Neil Finn
Engineer: Tchad Blake, Paul Kosky
Assistant Engineer: Rob Jaczko, Andrew Horne, Max Garcia
Mixer: Bob Clearmountain
Recorded between 1989 and 1991 at A&M Studios (LA), Periscope Studios (Melbourne), Ocean Way Studios (Hollywood) and Platinum Studios (Melbourne)
Released in July 1991 on Capitol Records
Running time: 48:11
Highest chart position UK: 6, US: 82, Australia: 2, Canada: 20

After the *Temple Of Low Men* tour ended, Neil and Tim Finn met to write some songs intended for a Finn Brothers album. Around the same time, Crowded House were preparing for their third release, as Capitol Records wanted to maintain the momentum hot on the heels of their first two successful albums. The melding of the two projects now seemed inevitable, as Neil explained to Radio New Zealand in 2016:

> Tim's inclusion in the band came together very naturally. Although Crowded House had begun to record an entire album before we decided to include Tim, what happened was that the songs that Tim and I had written demanded to be done and they started to be included on the Crowded House record. It became very obvious to all of us that the album would be very strong with both Tim and the songs he and I had written. It would be

> far less schizophrenic than it was when we were planning two records – a duo record and a Crowded House record. Figuring out when we were going to release them was becoming a nightmare, so it's been good for everybody.

Although *Woodface* is a lighter-sounding album overall, Neil and Tim have never been afraid to address difficult topics in their songs. Like the two albums that precede it, darkness hovers over the songs but never commands their identities. A catchy melody will lighten any load. The band continued to present themselves as light-hearted songsmiths, like modern-day Kiwi Marx Brothers but were committed to writing songs with depth, earnestness and sometimes even gravity.

Finn explained this paradox in the 2023 Zoom conversation:

> The juxtaposition of lyrical things … I guess I find the darker threads of living and relationships more interesting than naturally writing 'I love you, you love me' songs. Even though I feel those things, there's a slight awkwardness about it. I think I've had a few here and there that have been unequivocal, but I seem to operate best when exploring those moments of doubt and conflict and sadness with joy. That melancholy overtone; even when I was a teenager and didn't have a care in the world, I liked those kinds of songs.

'Chocolate Cake' (Neil Finn/Tim Finn)

Countless musicians from around the world have written songs about America as a promised land of sorts. Generally, these songs are tinged with an ironic realisation that all that glitters is, indeed, less than golden. Artists of the highest musical strata, including Elton John, The Rolling Stones and U2, have all contributed to this playlist with songs that declare their fascination with America or point out America's faults.

Add to this catalogue 'Chocolate Cake', an editorial on certain elite, entitled Americans and their appetite for overindulgence. The song is largely a laundry list of extravagance and excess, with special emphasis on the artifice heavily embedded in American culture and some of the people who partake in it. Obvious references include the spectacle of Broadway musicals, bogus artwork that looks genuine (and people's desperation to have a 'name' hanging on their living room wall), Andy Warhol again (see 'Mansion In The Slums'), celebrity impersonators, the lack of American health care, fast food culture and televangelism – all played to a 'sickly and sentimental' soundtrack.

The reference to Tammy Baker probably refers to Tammy Faye Bakker (with 2 Ks), the wife of televangelist Jim Bakker and his PTL club. She notoriously wept openly in every broadcast as she pleaded for donations to her husband's church. She became a cultural symbol of greed, fame and indulgence. Jim was charged with fraud and served eight years in prison. The couple divorced around the same time he was released.

It's not that 'Chocolate Cake' is particularly critical of American elitism, but rather, it's a tongue-in-cheek evaluation of how anyone, including those of us watching from the outside, could be seduced by the commercialism and sensationalism that permeates Western culture. It's why so many Americans refer to their home as 'the greatest country in the world' despite evidence to the contrary. If written today, it might include something about the nationalistic divisiveness now cleaving a fissure through the population.

So, the Finns remind us that 'We're all tempting fate, cars are shooting by with no number plates'. The wealthiest country in the world still has grave poverty and a problem with gun control that's killing their own citizens.

As the opener and lead single on *Woodface*, it signalled a new Crowded House in more than one way. The Finn brothers' reunion caused immediate shockwaves among Split Enz fans who might not have hopped onto the Crowded House bandwagon, assuming – hoping – that the quirkier, more arty flavours that Tim brought to that band would climb in through Crowded House's windows. 'Chocolate Cake' would have ticked those boxes with its stream-of-consciousness lyrics co-delivered by the brothers. Not to mention its densely produced soundscape utilising unpredictable guitar and keyboard sounds, extra voices (including some distant, distorted 'la-la-la's after the first chorus) and a killer harmonica solo by the late Australian bluesman Chris Wilson.

What this song lacks in melodic charm is made up for by its compact lyrical collage and slick production. With everything going on in this song, the band are tight and the individual playing is superb. It's an unusual song, to be sure, but it showcases a band at the top of their game.

'It's Only Natural' (Neil Finn/Tim Finn)

That quirkiness segues into the opening of 'It's Only Natural', beginning with a brief few seconds of scratches and honks before a guitar riff introduces the song proper. At a taut 3:32, it was the third *Woodface* single, released in December 1991.

Every line is sung in two-part harmony from start to finish, which is understandable, as the Finn brothers grew up singing together. In the context of Crowded House, what makes this unique is that it's difficult to determine which Finn is singing the melody. However, that remains largely immaterial as this melody functions largely because both vocal lines have equal importance.

Sometimes, as Neil and Tim suggest here, our fate is beyond our control. For better or worse, they say, we'll be together because that is what nature has intended. But it can also be 'circumstantial, it's nothing written in the sky'. Occasionally, we can start at one event in our life and trace its occurrence back to a particular decision we made, perhaps years earlier. And despite some lyrical references coming from a religious perspective – 'Man in a cage has made his confession' – there seems to be some doubt that religious faith is responsible for the natural state of finding love. Screw faith, if I'm going to go down on my knees, the narrator sings, it won't be in prayer but rather to beg you for a little you-know-what: 'Please let me have my way with you'.

The third verse references the apocalypse, by which time the connection has already been confirmed: 'You don't have to say, I know you're afraid. It's only natural…' Neil told the *Great Australian Albums* documentary in 2007:

> We were talking a lot at that time about subatomic particles and quarks. The first verse was very much influenced by that conversation – the rubbing together of spirituality and science.

'Fall At Your Feet' (Neil Finn)

Finn reflected on the song in the 2023 Zoom conversation:

> I had the chorus with a number of different verses. Mitchell kept pushing to get the right combination, and eventually, in the studio, I was playing a piece I had written as a teenager that he jumped on. It was a Eureka moment. We recorded the rhythm track 30 minutes later.

Showcasing another classic Neil Finn lyric, this initially sounds like a typical love song with the usual tropes: 'I'll be there when you call' and 'Let your tears rain down on me'. It's not until the bridge that we start to understand why the narrator is professing his love so vehemently. He's trying to help her through her pain, even though it seems he's the one to blame.

The song begins with a Finnian inconsistency. The narrator refers to 'her' in the opening two lines, then after a jarring bar of 2/4 ('Let it go'), he shifts perspective and begins singing to 'you'. It's as if he's thinking abstractly, deep inside his own thoughts about 'lying in the dark' close to her but feeling miles away. Then, he shifts to a more concrete reality, trying desperately to let go of his own insecurities. By the time they get together, he recognises, 'there's something in the way that you're talking, words don't sound right'. So, he falls flat at her feet to catch her tears.

In a catalogue of endless ear-friendly choruses, this may be one of the friendliest. There's great melodic movement up and down the scale, stark intervals that are easy to sing along with and lyrics that roll off the tongue. It's also at a tempo that chugs forward but doesn't race by – it lingers like a 'slow turning pain'.

Finn again utilises a shift from a minor key centre in the verse to a major one in the chorus. As a songwriting technique, he is quick to point out, as he did in the 2023 Zoom conversation, that although it's effective, it's nothing he views as particularly revolutionary:

> It's a simple trick to have a minor verse and a major chorus. I have ended up there on quite a few occasions. Songs like 'Fall At Your Feet' are a classic example of the difficult verse sentiment and then the offer of help, comfort and support in the chorus. That's a good place to be, I think.

The recording sounds like it was largely performed by the band live off the floor with only a few overdubs. This live sound gives it an organic feeling that can't be duplicated with the use of click tracks and production techniques.

A recording from an early rehearsal of the song shows how it evolved from having a strong chorus with a verse that didn't fit. The original verse became a new song, 'Left Hand', which later appeared on *Afterglow*.

'Tall Trees' (Neil Finn/Tim Finn)

We know that Neil and Tim's mother emigrated from Ireland to New Zealand, a journey that must have surely been exhausting, if not a bit harrowing. In 'Tall Trees', we can imagine 'a boy and girl arriving' in a new land where the search for a beacon or talisman might lead to an important first discovery in their new world – something to represent a claim staked on unfamiliar ground. A tall tree, where a home could be built under its shady boughs, might be just the object to write this story around.

Of course, the taller the tree, the deeper the roots. By the time they were writing the songs that were to become *Woodface* (and shortly after, the Finn brothers' first album as a duo, *Finn*), Neil was in his mid-30s and Tim was nearly 40. They'd started families of their own and had grown strong roots both in their home lives and in the community of music. It's no wonder, then, that these ideas crop up prominently in 'Tall Trees'.

'Remember when you were green ... You must keep running the distance', they sing together in a chorus that could use more of an injection of energy than it receives. Set to a 'Can't Carry On' tempo, the 'Tall Trees' melody is less interesting – less vertical (the melody stays fixed) – than most other Crowded House songs, yet its appeal is maintained by the running rhythm and some aggressive guitar work. The accented beats in each line of the chorus are the hook that the rest of the song hangs from.

In the midst of this genealogical bluster comes a moving, but not overly sentimental, bridge in which they reflect on where they came from: 'And the roses you grow have a powerful scent. They'll be breaking your heart by the morning'.

'Weather With You' (Neil Finn/Tim Finn)

If Neil was happy with the singalong chorus of 'Better Be Home Soon', he must have been absolutely euphoric with 'Weather With You'. The third single released from *Woodface*, it is arguably the single most earworm-worthy passage ever crafted by a Finn.

The single-phrase chorus lyric gets repeated with minor variations: 'Everywhere you go, you always take the weather with you'. But every memorable lyric needs a memorable melody. It starts on the pickup to beat one and lands on the word '...go' with the slightest anticipation of beat one. The melody, starting at the sixth note of the scale degree, descends diatonically to the root note as opposed to the opposite motion of the song's first line. The second line uses only the fourth, fifth and sixth notes of the scale degree, climbing up and then stepping back down. Again, minor variations occur in the repeated lines but with essentially the same notes. It's so simple and so effective. It's not the most beautiful or even interesting Crowded House melody – it's just the most memorable.

This song is written in an unusual form for a pop song: A B A C C C. In other words, verse-bridge-verse-chorus-chorus-chorus, with one of those false endings slipped in between the last two choruses.

Neil explained some of the song's beginnings in the *Great Australian Albums* documentary in 2007:

> 57 Mount Pleasant Street is a fictitious address as far as the number goes, but my sister used to live in a house on Mount Pleasant Road in Auckland and that's what we were thinking of when we wrote the song. It was just a good contrast to the theme of the song for it to be called Mount Pleasant Street because, really, it was about a guy who's totally wrapped up in melancholia, standing in his lounge feeling lost.

On an album bursting with tight, meandering harmonies, 'Weather With You' is a prime example of the Finn brothers' natural musical bond. Their two voices come together as one, creating a sound where it is nearly impossible to identify which Finn is singing which part. This is a rare and special gift, nurtured by a lifetime of singing together.

'Whispers And Moans' (Neil Finn)

A plaintive song that shows the frustration one can have with just trying to get through the day; times are tough for this protagonist. Maybe it's nuclear annihilation, high interest rates or – to read the song from a more recent vantage point – climate change. There's always something that threatens everything from the status quo to our very existence. But from Finn's perspective, the 'dull grey', the worries of the common man ('I will catch the taxi driver weeping like a wounded beast') and 'the clamour of the street' are all drowned out by the sounds of pleasure.

The chorus starts with the glorious statement, 'When I wake up in your room to share one piece of your life', then bows to the erotic sensations of 'your whispers and moans ... here you come to carry me home'. A heavier bridge suggests his heartbeat is racing. Indeed, the song feels as though it's speeding up, though it isn't. 'Love that sound. Time erase', he sings before once again waking up in her room. In a frantic coda, Finn rants about how we should cling to these beautiful moments so that, 'in a lifetime of suspicion', we are 'cleansed in a moment of recognition'. He goes on to allegedly include a reference to Alan Bond, a high-roller Australian businessman convicted of fraud.

If ever there was an example of bassist Nick Seymour's contribution to the Crowded House sound, 'Whispers And Moans' shines as one of the greatest.

The success of the intro alone is all down to the bass. His soul, r&b and Motown influences spring to the fore in this song, proving his dexterity as a musician and his invaluable role in the band. While Finn's songs can sometimes ring with esoteric qualities as he navigates the relationships between major and minor chords, with 7ths and 9ths peppering the changes – not to mention his exacting and sometimes dark lyrics – it's Seymour's bass lines that propel the songs into a groovier, more welcoming space for the listener. His natural feel, great sense of time and musical creativity are the unsung heroes of Crowded House, connecting viscerally, almost subliminally, to Finn's structures. To 'Whispers And Moans', Seymour brings the same elements he applies to, for example, 'Don't Dream It's Over': melodic bass that winds and weaves through the guitar's metronomic guitar strumming, a cohesive musical thread from start to finish and a playful jauntiness bouncing over the more sober hills and valleys.

'Four Seasons In One Day' (Neil Finn/Tim Finn)

For the *Great Australian Albums* documentary in 2007, Neil said:

> Tim and I were pretty mercurial and riding emotional rollercoasters all the time. So, it was a good description of our many moods, collectively and individually. The music for both 'Into Temptation' and 'Four Seasons In One Day' happened at the same time. They were part of the same piece at one point and are sister songs in tempo and atmosphere.

These are men in touch with their emotions. Whether they are singing about themselves or others, the lyrics in this song prove their ability to cope with and articulate complex feelings and empathy, all without being explicit about what the problems are.

In this song, they identify how one can feel elements of both despair and joy at the same time: 'The sun shines on the black clouds hanging over the domain'. They acknowledge the occasional need to put on a brave face ('Smiling as the shit comes down'), remind us of the power of listening ('You can tell a man from what he has to say') and rely on the notion that, despite our best efforts, we can be a slave to our emotions ('Like all the things you can't explain, four seasons in one day').

The fourth and final single from *Woodface*, these verses sound undeniably melancholy, with the melody using every note of the E minor scale. The chorus then lifts – in a surprising C major – with a soaring reminder that happy times are just around the corner: 'Blood dries up like rain'. Maybe it's faith, or maybe it all starts with the gentle acknowledgement of being human and simply recognising our inability to speak emotionally about our own pain, flaws and inefficiencies.

This is a vast and wildly meandering exploration of a phrase commonly used to discuss the weather. A mainly strummed arrangement with some nice vocals, brushes and occasional piano, the intensity lifts in the chorus but never loses its gentleness.

'There Goes God' (Neil Finn/Tim Finn)

There is not a lot of mystery to this song, but knowing the Finns were raised in a God-fearing Christian home suggests they've had the occasional conversation about God's existence. Perhaps as men of faith and artists, the Finns considered the possibility of God walking among us.

This song might be written from the perspective of a priest who is having his own moment of doubt: 'What'll I tell him when he comes to me for absolution?' What kind of inner turmoil might a man of the cloth endure if faced with the prospect of having to hear God's confession? In the greatest religious irony, could he be banished to the eternal Hellfires for providing bad counsel to God?

They're some of the same questions asked by XTC in 'Dear God', John Lennon in 'God', Joan Osbourne in 'One Of Us' and countless others. But it has more of the spirit of Elvis Costello's 'God's Comic', which gives God uncomfortably human characteristics: 'And if you know me why don't you tell me what I'm thinking'. The rousing chorus is practically heretical: 'Hey, don't look now but there goes God, in his sexy pants and his sausage dog'.

Another terrific Chris Wilson harmonica performance peppers the arrangement that is otherwise straightforward in a driving mid-tempo beat. During the coda, a call and response is used like a congregation's voice echoing the incantation coming from the altar: 'There goes God. Check your hat in at the stand. There goes God. Hey I'd like to shake his hand...'

'Fame Is' (Neil Finn)

The End-Time Handmaidens (And Servants) is a small Catholic sect rooted in rural America that appears to combine new-age spiritualism with feminism and Messianic Christianity. Its founder, Gwen Shaw – a soft-spoken, elfin Canadian woman – has been called, among other things, a false prophet. This is just the kind of scenario Neil Finn would find absolutely fascinating: 'Love children of the new age, just a hippie with a weekly wage', he sings.

If one's quest for fame is driven by the desire to be adored, as many might argue, then surely, in Finn's mind, it's a kind of spiritual faith: 'You follow the science of love, wave the magic wand and hang on'. The final words Finn screams at the end seem to come from a place of experience – his own fame: 'And all of your stars will fall. And all of your spells will break. So look out for number one'. Be careful what you wish for, he cautions, because, in the end, you only have yourself – your own soul and your own conscience – to rely on. Some people spend a lifetime searching for the right God to pray to, the right temple to worship in and the best crystals to rub, only to come up empty in the end. Generation after generation have tried and failed, he suggests: 'All the lives written on your face can't fill the canyons of your mind'. Can fame fill those holes? Isn't fame itself a kind of religion, with its idol worship and alabaster pedestals?

At less than two and a half minutes, this is the most brisk and one of the most rhythmically relentless songs in the Crowded House canon. For such a short song, it manages to cram in a full load: verse-chorus-verse-chorus-instrumental break-bridge-guitar solo-chorus-coda. Hester's double-time drumming ensures there's no lingering over any section, as Finn sounds breathless by the end. Like 'There Goes God', 'When You Come' and others, 'Fame Is' comes from a perspective of growing up in an environment of religious guidance.

'All I Ask' (Neil Finn/Tim Finn)

'All I ask is to live each moment free from the last'. A sentiment that is straight to the point: live for today, try not to get weighed down by choices you made before (even if they helped propel you to where you are now) and keep moving forward. Like Robert Frost's celebrated poem 'The Road Not Taken', this carries a message of no regret and straying 'far from familiar things'. Tim Finn sings about going down an unfamiliar path, even if it leads to 'nowhere in particular'. This could be a direct reference to his choice to join Crowded House, putting his own solo career on hold, and it might have been the exact same philosophy that prompted him to leave the band in the middle of their subsequent tour.

The use of strings sets a mood that matches the lyrical content. It is both romantically nostalgic and cinematically prescient, capturing a sound that could easily have come from Nelson Riddle's orchestra in the 1950s. With the release of *Woodface* in 1991 at the height of the flourishing era of Grunge, the choice to use a 22-piece orchestra – and virtually no other instruments (Seymour's bass is present and a tiny bit of guitar and percussion can be heard) – should be seen as radical. Then again, George Michael's use of a jazz quartet in 'Kissing A Fool', released three years earlier, might have set a precedent for pop acts stretching the sound of the 1990s.

Tim's strong vocal performance is sincere and intimate. For an album rich with the Finn Brothers' harmony, there is a sparse use of it here. The song peaks at around the 3:00 mark as the Finns sing in harmony on the penultimate 'free from the last'. The counterpoint on the word 'last', sounding very much like it might have been a passage destined for the strings, is one of the highlights of *Woodface*.

'As Sure As I Am' (Neil Finn)

A mid-tempo waltz, this song is emblematic of Finn's penchant for lilting, vertical, McCartney-esque melodies. Its sentiment is equally reminiscent of the former Beatle, who often wrote about the good fortune of just being alive, the glories of the world, the people in it and, above all, love. 'Living', as our narrator sings here, 'is luxury' as he delivers a monumental sign of adoration: 'I want everything you throw out. I'll do anything you want to'.

The bass and keyboard stay out of each other's way in the verses like they're having a conversation. Los Lobos' David Hidalgo's accordion provides lovely colour to what is otherwise an ordinary but enjoyable arrangement.

Finn calls the song 'a tongue-in-cheek jab at apathy and indifference' on his website, but there is genuine joy in the chorus, sung by someone so certain of his love and how it allows him to find his footing over the broken ground: 'I couldn't care less for what might go wrong'. While some writers might baulk at the explicit sentiment here, Finn gets away with it by inserting happiness into the middle of the very things that could conspire to make him unhappy: 'And I'm as happy as sin in a fear shaken world'.

This joy is assisted by the modulation in key. The verses start in a bright C# major (the original demo was in Bb but was altered, probably at the suggestion of producer Froom, to increase its brightness) before modulating to a C major chorus – one half-step down from the verse – on 'I am as sure as I am'. This simple modulation takes the chorus to a particularly transcendent level, giving the sense that it is floating above the rest of the song.

'Italian Plastic' (Paul Hester)

If it hadn't been listed on the album's liner notes, there would be no reason to believe this wasn't another Finn Brothers composition. The humour and turns of phrase echo 'Chocolate Cake' and the Finns' Split Enz era. The chorus resounds with melody and sentiment that resonates with the Crowded House ethos, now deep into its third album.

However, it was drummer Paul Hester's first solely composed song to make it onto a Crowded House album. Considering the prolific output by both Neil and Tim, it's a wonder that any other songwriter could burst through with a song to meet the standard. This speaks to the strength of 'Italian Plastic' as a song worthy of this band.

Even before it was recorded, 'Italian Plastic' was included in the live shows on the *Temple Of Low Men* tour, typically with Hester leaping around the stage like a schoolboy hopped up on Skittles during the double-time outro ('Who you gonna take to the ball tonight?'). No doubt, the overall audience reception encouraged the band to record it for the next album.

Hester's lyrics could easily have come from Neil's pen. While he admits to being silly, immature and having bad taste in gifts, our narrator still professes undying devotion to the one he loves. 'When you wake up with me, I'll be your glass of water' is a beautiful metaphor, no matter how thirsty you are.

'She Goes On' (Neil Finn)

Neil Finn had already proven his penchant for writing about emotional topics in songs like 'Hole In The River', 'Love This Life' and more. Written at the request of a friend, 'She Goes On' is a wistful but not solemn memory of a dear one. The inclusion of tender and beautiful imagery clings to the age-old philosophy that death is a part of life (*memento mori*) and that, depending on one's beliefs, we will all be together eventually. There is comfort in that reminder and, no doubt, for Finn, comfort in expressing that conviction when grieving a loss.

Finn references the people and places close by to keep the memory alive. We can imagine him sitting in a forest clearing in the mountains near his childhood home in New Zealand, strumming his guitar as he reflects on his friend. 'In her soft wind I will whisper, in her warm sun I will glisten', he sings, feeling her presence among the beauty that nature offers. He acknowledges the circle of life as children paint pictures of 'ladders to heaven', their own memories fresh and fragile.

In the end, we are reminded that, for many people, immortality is expressed through memories, laughter and tears.

'How Will You Go' (Neil Finn/Tim Finn)

A drinking song and a cautionary tale all in one. Writing from multiple perspectives, we hear this story about a dangerously committed alcoholic through the eyes of those around him as well as through his own eyes. The second verse alone houses a balanced perspective in four short lines. Our stupefied protagonist admits, 'I fell over on the couch again ...', before suggesting that there is a silver lining: 'But you know not all sleep is wasted'. The verse continues with a critical voice in the middle of this intervention: 'Your dreams are alcohol inspired', ensuring the dreamer recognises the crutch they are relying on. 'I can't find a better way to face it', he responds earnestly.

This song could be sung by two singers in a conversation between someone in a desperate state and the person – or people – intent on preventing the downward spiral. There is recognition here that the alcoholic is slowly killing himself. 'How will you go?' is not just a question to clarify how they might get home that night ('Drive through the wind and the rain'), nor is it a concerned voice asking about this individual's future. Rather, it explicitly asks for a prediction about how they will die.

Yet, despite the darkness of the lyric, in the hands of the Finn melody masters, there is a lightness of touch. The song bounces in 6/8, with some lovely guitar fills popping up throughout. The chorus is as much of a sing-along as any Crowded House song. You can imagine a pub full of sailors swaying back and forth in unison, their steins of ale aloft as they chant together: 'How will you go? How will you go?'

The bridge provides an opportunity for the alcoholic to ask for a second chance: 'And you know I'll be fine, just don't ask me how it's going. Gimme time, gimme time'. This is followed by an instrumental break that leads to the final choruses. The abrupt ending comes too soon by sing-along standards.

It is a well-earned album closer, even following the penultimate track's similar subject matter. But wait – there's more...

'I'm Still Here' (Paul Hester/Neil Finn/Nick Seymour)
Like most hidden songs, 'I'm Still Here' remained unlisted and uncredited for many years. Once the final chords of 'How Will You Go' have faded away, listeners are pummelled by a thud and distorted electric guitar after 30 seconds of silence. Following a faint 'two, three, four' count-in, the band kick in with a bass-heavy groove and a steady chant of 'I'm still here', over which Hester extemporises appropriate responses, including 'I won't go away' and 'I've come to rain on your parade'.

It's a hidden track wrapped up in a one-line joke. The album's not over yet, the band haven't left the building – they're still here, we get it. Although it's credited to the band, it is almost certainly owed to Hester, whose sense of humour was widely witnessed in the band's videos (such as 'Something So Strong' and 'Chocolate Cake') and live appearances and who had already shown his inclination toward off-the-wall ditties ('Italian Plastic'). It resulted from a band jam with Hester on guitar and Finn on drums. Hester said in 1997 (neilfinn.com):

> That generally happens because Neil goes to play the drums. When Neil feels that he's got one in him, he'll go play his drum beat and there's not much we can do with that. And 'I'm Still Here' reared its ugly head. When we recorded it, it was the same feeling. It was one of those songs where you couldn't really do a rendition of it. You had to immerse yourself back into the horror of the original recording.

Ultimately, 'I'm Still Here' began showing up listed on re-releases and streaming platforms, with some questionably listing it as a medley with 'How Will You Go'.

Together Alone (1993)

Personnel
Neil Finn: guitar, piano, keyboards, lead and backing vocals
Nick Seymour: bass, backing vocals
Paul Hester: drums, percussion, lead and backing vocals
Mark Hart: keyboards, guitar, lap steel guitar, mandolin, backing vocals
Additional musicians:
Eddie Rayner: keyboards
Noel Crombie: percussion
Geoffrey Hales: percussion
Tim Finn: backing vocals
Sharon Finn: backing vocals
Dror Erez: accordion
Te Waka Huia Cultural Group Choir: choral vocals
Joe, Tereo, Martie, Jamee, Benjamin: log drummers
Clyde Dixon, Stephen Bremner, Laura Astridge, David Bremner, Shaun Jarrett: brass band
Producer: Youth
Engineer: Greg Hunter
Additional Engineers: Angus Davidson, Chris Corr, Graeme Myhre, Kalju Tonuma, Nick Morgan, Dugald McAndrew
Programmer: Matt Austin
Mixer: Bob Clearmountain
Recorded between 1992 and 1993 at Nigel and Jody Horrocks' house (Karekare, NZ), Periscope Studios (Melbourne) and Platinum Studios (Melbourne)
Released in October 1993 on Capitol Records
Running time: 51:32
Highest chart position UK: 4, US: 73, Australia: 2, Canada: 18
All songs by Neil Finn, unless otherwise specified

> *Together Alone* is my favourite Crowded House album. It was a potent mix of influences on that record and it kept everything in a nice ethereal plane.
> **Neil Finn in an interview with Zane Lowe from Apple Music in 2021**

This is a transition album in many ways. Tim had left the band, but their global status and reputation had skyrocketed. Having the opportunity to record anywhere with anyone became almost overwhelming. Crowded House were suddenly romanced by some of the most well-known producers, including Steve Lillywhite (U2, XTC, Talking Heads and more), with whom they would later work. After meeting with several potential producers, they decided they got along best with Youth (The Fireman, The Verve). Ultimately, they desired to simplify the recording process by minimising the glossy temptations of grand studios and over-production.

Talking about the album with Radio New Zealand's Jeremy Ansell, who also co-produced the Deluxe Editions released in 2016, the band said:

> Seymour: To Youth's credit, he seemed to be aware of the alternative style of formulating arrangements through live mixing from the DJ culture or the House culture, where you keep things very modal and do a board mix, which is also in that reggae dub style.
>
> Finn: Yeah, we were excited about that whole area. That's why we used him. We quite liked the idea of being deconstructed by someone from the dub culture.
>
> Seymour: And that really assisted Paul. Even though he struggled with Youth on occasion, he really saw that side of seeing drums texturally and he was excited by a lot of those board mixes that Youth did on jams that we had.

To that end, after years based in Melbourne and Los Angeles, where the bulk of their first three albums were recorded, they rented a house in Karekare, a remote settlement in a coastal valley to the west of Auckland, New Zealand. The result is an album imbued with the aura of the valley: simple, organic songs that reflect on humanity's minor significance in an infinite universe.

However, it was not a perfect time for the band. Hester grew increasingly uneasy with his role – and with the innate claustrophobia experienced while spending nearly ten years with the same group of people – and he angrily left the recording studio on more than one occasion. It signalled the tentative future of Crowded House. Finn summarised the experience during the 2023 Zoom conversation:

> We decided we'd go back to New Zealand to record. I liked the idea of the reconnection with the spiritual home. Having come through very similar situations up until then, we took a gamble on the producer, partly because of his completely different manner and thoughts about recording. We also reached the point where the sort of music we wanted to make was a little deeper and denser. We became a jamming band and wanted to hit something different. It was a very creative time, but there were weird energies around, which possibly made good music as well. Five relationships in the band and surrounding community broke up during the making of that album.

'Kare Kare' (Neil Finn/Nick Seymour/Mark Hart/Paul Hester)
From the first bar of the song, we are introduced to a new sound in the band's aural lexicon: Mark Hart's lap steel guitar. It's a sound that would become a major source of colour and texture throughout this album and the next two. As Mitchell Froom's contribution on keyboards had filled in the

trio's gaps previously, so now did Hart's steel. Moreover, his significance was so great that Crowded House were now officially a quartet.

It couldn't be too difficult to imagine showing up at the Karekare house – having carried the recording console up a hill to set up their ersatz studio – and immediately wanting to capture the mood musically and collectively. Film footage shows the dramatic views in all directions from the modern structure tucked into the side of the valley. The first impressions alone must have been overwhelming. It's the first time that all four members of Crowded House are credited as songwriters.

This is the country, after all, that Peter Jackson, the New Zealand-born director, used to film the *Lord Of The Rings* trilogy. These lyrics capture the level of fantasy this magical location would inspire. From their vantage point, our narrator is 'standing on a wave', 'lying in a cave', marvelling at 'a valley lit by the moon ... in a long-forgotten place'. It's Tolkien-level stuff.

While the charm of their new surroundings is palpable, arguably the most interesting part of the song is the perspective (most likely Finn's) of being back in New Zealand after a significant time away. Though he's long acknowledged it as his home – proudly so – he'd been eager to find other places to set up shop, record and tour. Now, being drawn back to his homeland, he recognises that 'this is the only place that I always run from'. Why did he run? And why has he returned? There is comfort in returning to a 'long-forgotten place', particularly when seeing it again through new eyes.

The chorus – if you can call it that – is subdued in 'Kare Kare'. It doesn't pop out of the song like so many Crowded House choruses do. Listeners who might be compelled to sing along with 'Weather With You' are less likely to join in with the more poetic lyrics on offer here. Unlike many memorable choruses that might modulate up, or at least rise up the scale melodically, this one steps down in an acknowledged resignation of returning home. Finn's often-used trick of inserting a major chord into the chorus of a song based in a minor key was eschewed here, preferring instead to go from E minor to A minor, hanging onto the melancholy a few bars longer. In fact, only the bridge, when Finn admits he's always running from this place, switches to a major key centre. He's owning his admission and, in doing so, perhaps, suggesting that his travels are not over.

'In My Command'

This is another biting example of Finn approaching a narrative from two complementary perspectives. It's a song about losing and gaining control of a situation. First, the narrator asks the subject to let down their guard, which is clearly a difficult prospect. Not only that, but he's suggesting going even further: surrender. There is even the suggestion of finding some benefit in that: 'It's just a fear of losing control you know so well. Don't miss it when the moment comes, be submissive just this once'. Then, once he has convinced his subject to yield, he brandishes his authority like Zeus from a mountaintop. In the haunting and slightly off-putting chorus – where his delivery of the lyric feels like it's stumbling, unsure of his footing – he claims the power to which he feels beholden: 'I would love to trouble you in your time of need. Lose your way, it's a pleasure when you're in my command'. As the song continues, the narrator breaks down the will of his partner – and sings calmingly – ensuring first that 'you're responsible for everything', only to be followed quickly by 'you're not responsible for anything'.

In typical Crowded House fashion, the sinister undertones of this song are masked by the catchy melody and Finn's warm vocals. Even in the verses where he uses his harder-edged voice (a la 'Love You 'Til The Day I Die', 'Kill Eye', etc.), we are still soothed by the knowledge that it's only Neil, the soft-spoken minstrel who serenades us with his lilting melodies. Not every singer can get away with presenting these harsh realities in such a sweet way.

Instrumentally, the band play a chugging opening riff – a rockier version of ABBA's 'Does Your Mother Know' – which, when it returns later, is combined with a dissonant guitar solo leading directly into the harsh: 'Desolate in anger or safe in isolation, you're about to be the victim of a holy visitation'. Finn has never sounded so threatening. He then magically provides the soothing balm in another chorus and coda. He is, once again, Jekyll and Hyde, yin and yang, blaming and mollifying all at once.

'Nails In My Feet'

This is one of Finn's most flawless lyrics, which uses an extended metaphor throughout. It is summed up tidily in the first two lines: 'My life is a house. You crawl through the window'. In other words, I am stuck in my walls, closed and unreachable, but you have managed to burrow inside and find the core of me. It was released as the second single from *Together Alone*. Sharing a tempo and feel with 'Better Be Home Soon', it may have seemed a natural choice for a single.

Maybe it's love ('You my companion'), or maybe the 'you' in this song is an actual saviour, a personal messiah who selflessly wears 'the nails on your feet'. Either way, the narrator seems genuinely touched by the efforts 'You' made to reach him. Finn's velvety tones express the emotional release of being unbound from a prison of his own making. He has been taken from a place where 'there is no connection', where he hides from 'a conversation I can't face', to a place where he is seen, understood and not taken for granted. To have been locked inside for so long, even by his own hand, only to be lured out by the love of another person would be nothing short of an emancipation.

Still, the sense of freedom does not come instantly to our protagonist. The first chorus is sung tentatively, almost dubiously ('Who is that calling?') as he comes to recognise the relief his companion is bringing. He needs convincing to lose his inhibitions, which might take much longer than this intervention had been scheduled for. Eventually, however, he succumbs to 'total surrender', either because 'You' has managed to drag him outside or because he finally understands that the only way to receive help is to allow himself to obtain it completely. When he finally sings, 'And it brings me relief', as the final lyric, the feeling of liberation is palpable. He repeats the refrain another four times as the song fades.

The song is in C minor, but the chordal movement takes it somewhere unexpected. It bounces around cleverly and seamlessly until, as the song fades, the band vamp on the Bb. So the fadeout is rooted a full step below the C minor key of the song, but it sounds neither awkward nor unnatural. Rather, it sounds like relief.

'Black And White Boy'

Finn reflected on this song in the 2023 Zoom conversation:

> It's always nice when a song has a couple of angles going in them. We had a Dalmatian, Lester, and a poet friend called Sam Hunt. He would come around for long dinners, and in the course of regaling us with long stories and poems, Lester would be wandering around our legs and Sam would go, 'Black and white boy, fuck off.' So it became a catchphrase. Obviously, it was kind of about Paul – he was quite extreme in certain ways. On that record, there were times when he'd go from being the greatest fun and company you could imagine to being quite dark. There is a lot of hidden anger and energy in there, so the song is definitely connected with the idea that somebody is quite strongly swinging from pole to pole.

It must be terribly frustrating and very saddening to witness helplessness in people you know and love. Those looking in at mental illness from the outside may struggle to be anything but observers. No doubt, as Finn witnessed his friend Paul's struggles, he responded the only way he knew how to. Finn couldn't have stated more clearly what he observed in his friend: the unbridled joy he could bring to a room superimposed onto the dark landscape painted by his inner demons. And, perhaps more to the point, grappling with transitioning between the two extremes.

Wouldn't it be great to say to a dear friend, reassuringly, 'Colour me in, whatever mood I'm in' or 'You make fools of the liars and creeps, put a rose in my cheeks'? Undoubtedly, there is joy and love shared between these friends that any amount of turmoil could scarcely tarnish. Still, when he steps back and watches his friend's inevitable transformation, the incredulity in what he sees might naturally make him doubt the friendship altogether. This, one could easily assume, is one of the real tragedies of bipolar disorder, which Paul suffered from: 'When demons have climbed on your back, you are vicious and quick to attack'.

However, even if true friends don't know how to communicate it, they are there to help. It seems here that Finn tries to reach out to Paul with a simple, 'Do you really, really think I don't know?' There is evidence of this maddening vexation in the wordless vocalising that starts at 3:36 of 'Black And White Boy'. Finn's altruistic desires mean nothing if they are not willingly received.

It's another pure example of a Crowded House arrangement meshing neatly with a Neil Finn lyric. The melody makes great use of minor second, major second and minor third intervals, all sounding tight and creating necessary tension. The arrangement is appropriately thick with rasping guitars and pounding bass and drums, but the track is still easy to sing along with.

'Fingers Of Love'

Crepuscular rays are typically seen at twilight when the sun has just dipped over the western horizon and its residual light sifts through low-hanging clouds. The rays of light poke through like fingers reaching down to stroke the earth. Some people refer to them as God's rays for obvious reasons. Or, if you're Neil Finn on holiday in Jamaica and have just enjoyed smoking some of the homegrown vegetation, they can be fingers of love, as he told the *New Zealand Herald* in 2001:

> Naturally, I was enjoying some really good quality Jamaican weed whilst sitting out on the balcony with my guitar as I watched the sun go down with these extraordinary shafts of light coming through the clouds.

He then proceeded to write about what those shafts of light looked and felt like to him: 'A light that falls through the cracks', 'I hear the endless murmur, every blade of grass that shivers in the breeze' and 'Colour is its own reward'. He sings about being immobilised by these things around him while the 'fingers of love move down' from on high – God's touch continuing to create his world as he sits solitary on his balcony, guitar in hand. He can't look up or look back; he can't be helped because this light is busy crafting everything around him 'beneath the dying rays of the sun'. It's a simple – if slightly spaced-out – perspective on one specific moment captured by a songwriter sensitive to such moments.

Released as a single in the UK, Finn is quick to acknowledge the sexual overtones in the lyric – as was the case with 'When You Come' – and makes no apologies. From the *New Zealand Herald* in 2001:

> Clearly, I'm not so stupid that I wouldn't consider that some people might see it that way, but in truth, the reality of both of those songs was not a particularly sexy moment. 'Fingers Of Love' is more about blitzing out on nature but if there's another angle, you play it up.

The song proceeds with a minimalist arrangement, generally relying on strumming guitar, Mark Hart's lap steel, minimal bass and percussion, and, low in the mix, a steady drone. However, the intensity builds as the 'fingers of love move down', rising during the bridge ('From the cradle to the grave') and through a short lap steel solo. The entire song relies on a mellifluous, if enigmatic, spacy vibe that remains constant throughout and seems appropriate, given the song's inspiration. An early demo reveals an arrangement more akin to the band's Motown influences, which, in all likelihood, would have been quelled by producer Youth.

'Pineapple Head'

It's difficult to interpret 'Pineapple Head' living anywhere other than in a fantasy world. On the surface, it's about a detective in the clutches of a fever trying to find details about a woman he used to know. In the midst of his memories is a spinning pineapple head, which, though vivid, stands out as something of a mystery. This could refer to the spiny leaves of an actual pineapple or, as depicted on the cover of the single released in 1994, a person – the detective perhaps – with a pineapple for a head. Either way, it seems to have no bearing on anything.

Finn explained to Radio New Zealand's Jeremy Ansell in 2016 for the Deluxe Edition release:

> My son Liam, who was a boy at the time, was delirious with a fever. I was tending to him, mopping his brow with a wet flannel. He started spouting these great lines: 'Detective is flat'. 'Getaway car'. All these great images. And I went downstairs and wrote the lines down and wrote 'Pineapple Head' on the piano shortly after he'd been spouting these great, delirious images. I neglected my duties as a father but got a good song out of it – we're still arguing about the publishing.

It's Finn's 'Lucy In The Sky With Diamonds' moment. Whatever your interpretation of this song's perplexing lyrics, musically, it is one of the album's most accessible. The chorus melody is one of the catchiest on *Together Alone* thanks in part to the application of some of Finn's favourite intervals: the minor seventh ('If you choose') and the sixth ('to take that path') sung over the sudden shift to a minor chord. These lines are followed by the intoxicating 'I will play you like a shark and I'll clutch at your heart' over some terrific chordal movement, all winding up with a well-timed suspended chord and resolution under 'to inflame you'.

As usual, the arrangement of this song would be less satisfying if not for Seymour's stellar bass line. In a band whose main songwriter is often compared to The Beatles, here, Seymour is at his most McCartney-esque, finding a bass line that is a melody of its own. During the verses, he barely touches the root notes, preferring to dance above them like he's avoiding touching lava. Other comparisons must surely include Chris Squire, Graham Maby and Sting.

Played in a straightforward 6/8, 'Pineapple Head' shares a few features with The Beatles' 'Norwegian Wood'. Aside from the time signature and almost identical tempo, the guitar intros create a similar mood. As George Harrison added sitar to John Lennon's guitar to highlight the melody, Hart added a mandolin (played in concert on an electric 12-string guitar) to Finn's acoustic guitar. Both songs take advantage of modulating between major and minor chords to highlight section changes and delineate shifts in the narrative. Neither song uses much percussion, if any, as both rely instead on the acoustic instruments and chordal movement to set the tone.

'Locked Out'

'Locked Out' is a relentless song that never wavers from its motivation to unlock itself. It's a clock stuck in a moment, forever ticking the same minute over and over. The band sound at their heaviest since 'Fame Is' as they hope to burst through the walls that lock them inside. Like the video that accompanied this single's release in February 1994, which shows the band members running through the streets of a small Welsh town, never seeming to get anywhere, the song doesn't give up or give in – it persistently pursues its deepest desires to an almost quixotic degree.

Finn's vocals ring with desperation as he declares his intention to break through the walls that separate him from the one he loves. Based in E major, Finn's melody never strays too far from the root note. He sticks close to home lest his love chooses to call for him and he's not there. This man will go to great lengths to win back the woman he loves. Of particular delight: 'And the hills are as soft as a pillow, and they cast a shadow on my bed'. Throughout, we see the man's perspective 'in a shack as remote as a mansion' as he patiently does what he deems necessary to reach the object of his love. She's always there on his mind, keeping him focused and dedicated to his task: 'Every night I circle like the moon. And it's an act of simple devotion, but it can take forever when you've got something to prove'.

Finn claims he was inspired to write the song after reading the novel *Bliss* by Peter Carey, part of which involves the hero of the story pursuing the woman he loves over many years by cultivating the plants that help create her favourite honey. As he told Jeremy Ansell for the Deluxe Edition in 2016:

> I was taken by that endurance aspect of love and not allowing yourself to be shut out forever. It's about trying to win back somebody's affection and realising that it's going to take a lot of time and a lot to prove.

While 'Locked Out' adheres to a fairly standard form – A B A B solo C A B – there is little to distinguish verse from chorus. As Finn's writing gathered more sophistication, he seemed to care less and less about such things, preferring to alter lyrics in repeated musical sections, making each chorus unique. This A section might be the chorus, as A2 and A3 are the same.

However, the change into the B section – shifting from E major to B major – sounds completely chorus-worthy.

'Private Universe'

Finn explores one of the pleasures of being an adult: nostalgically reflecting on the innocent virtues of childhood, those moments before the pebbles of obligations and priorities began filtering into your pockets and before there was a need to learn the skills of making small talk or keeping to a schedule.

For some, as Finn reflects on in this song, it might be as simple as climbing a tree. From that perspective, he is both rooted and weightless, and in those moments, he creates the impossible: a place for privacy and a vantage point for the universal. Finn remembers running for shelter to his chosen hiding spot, which sounds as if he might have been fleeing something ('…lift the curse'). Essentially, 'It feels like nothing matters in our private universe' sounds more like a place he would prefer to escape to. As an adult, with the benefit of hindsight, he shares, 'I have all I want, is that simple enough?' After all these years, he wonders if his place of simplicity has endured or changed, but in the end, he still clings to that memory which belongs to him alone: 'And it's a pleasure that I have known. And it's a treasure that I have gained'. As Finn told the *New Zealand Herald* in 2001:

> I don't know that it has a clear narrative, but it has a deep sense of atmosphere. Songs are an alternative reality, or they should be.

Still, there is a real sense of looking back, which, in Finn's case, means rural New Zealand. Not coincidentally, then, several Māori musicians were brought in to play traditional log drums, providing an even stronger feeling of roots to the song. Coupled with the steady A minor drone (a low string pad), the foundation is set for the atmospheric arrangement.

Released as a single in Australia at a radio-friendly 3:59, the album edit is the first Crowded House song to breach the five-minute threshold, clocking in at an epic 5:37. The track opens with sounds of the city: cars, trains, people. This is what the narrator is trying to escape from as the log drummers lead his dreamy recollection. An almost unrecognisable electric guitar chimes in the background and backing vocals fill out the fantasy. The syncopated groove is maintained right through to the fadeout.

'Walking On The Spot'

An early demo of this song, recorded in California when Neil and Paul were barely even the Mullanes, has an arrangement that would suit any Split Enz album: bouncy, quirky and a little bit odd. It sounds as if the light musical motif is used to defy the gravity of the lyrics – a cross between REM's 'Everybody Hurts' and Enz's 'Six Months In A Leaky Boat'. That the song was reimagined about a decade later in a more suitable style shows Finn's maturity as an artist and his willingness to take off his mask.

'Walking On The Spot' could be one of Finn's most introspective songs to date. In the context of *Together Alone,* it can also be seen as a companion piece to 'Nails In My Feet'. Both songs are sung by a solitary character afraid or unable to step out from a kind of sanctuary – a place to hide from their unbearable realities. Where 'Nails In My Feet' allows a companion to enter and offer relief, 'Walking On The Spot' makes no such allowance.

The protagonist of this song is treading water after succumbing to 'the dark hole' that sometimes sucks him in. Maybe it's the same abyss from 'Black And White Boy'. He is surviving, which is not the same as living, but despite the unwillingness to emerge from his den, he appears committed to providing, if only to himself, proof of life: 'Walking on the spot to show that I'm alive'.

In the chorus, Finn wants us to know that for every dark night, the sun will come up in the morning. More importantly, we should be able to be more honest with ourselves about the things we do and think: 'The world is somehow different, you have all been changed before my very eyes'. The music reflects this optimistic moment. During the verses, his melody descends at the end of each line, but in the chorus, his melody ascends as if rising out of the darkness. It's a simple but effective musical trick that Finn uses along with the minimal arrangement of piano, accordion, bass, brushes on snare and vocals.

'Distant Sun'

Now on the fourth album released by his second successful band, the 33-year-old Finn had proven himself effortlessly skilled at writing complete, adventurous and memorable three-and-a-half-minute songs. So it's less of a criticism and more of a curiosity that 'Distant Sun' sounds like the first time he set out to deliberately write a hit song – and, indeed, it was a hit. This first single from *Together Alone* rose in the charts to as high as number four in Canada, number five in New Zealand and number 13 in the US.

It's not that it's a bad song, far from it. 'Distant Sun' was a deserved hit, regardless of how deliberate Finn was about its creation. In the context of *Together Alone*, owing to the fact it falls amid some of the more esoteric Crowded House songs ever put to tape, it is given a more pronounced mainstream punch. It also features the great opening line: 'Tell me all the things you would change, I don't pretend to know what you want'. No matter what you hear, it wouldn't take a seasoned A&R guy to finger 'Distant Sun' as a song ready to hit the airwaves. It's immediately radio-friendly, sounding very much like a quartet simply playing their instruments with very few overdubs (perhaps only backing vocals and some guitar).

Thematically, the song doesn't stray far from the common 'You're great, I'm a loser' songwriting trope. According to Finn, the song was born out of a conversation about the Pleiades, a star cluster often referred to as the Seven Sisters. From there, it isn't difficult to perceive how Finn's creative imagination and singular perspective on love songs would end up with 'Distant Sun'. He has composed a jolly, upbeat melody that underscores the rather stern lyrics about love for someone who is, literally, out of this world. That this love seems to be unrequited is irrelevant to the singer, who admits, 'It's easy to forget what you learned, waiting for the thrill to return'. During those rare moments 'whenever I am by your side', the feeling he gets is astronomical, showered by the 'dust from a distant sun' even though he knows he is unable to return the satisfaction. Still, at the very least, 'I offer love' – it's the bare minimum, but it's all the currency he holds.

In the bridge, it's all laid on the line: 'And I'm lying on the table, washed out in a flood. Like a Christian fearing vengeance from above'. Love is love; eternal damnation be damned.

'Catherine Wheels' (Neil Finn/Tim Finn/Nick Seymour)
The Māori strum makes another return in this saga of Catherine and Claude, a couple caught in the age-old struggle for fidelity and happiness. Claude is unhappy and looks for alternative companionship 'to stroke the right nerve'. It's not that Catherine doesn't mind, but she's been ready for this moment. 'She was always the first to say gone' and now is the time to make good on her promise. She gets on her wheels and takes off. It's a satisfying play on words that Finn uses here. Famously, a Catherine wheel is a firework that spins around, pinwheel style, using the power of its own streaming pyrotechnics. It is at once in control and wildly free, as is Catherine, the protagonist of this song. First, she gets the idea that it's time to leave, like gears turning in her head: 'Whose needs do I serve, as Catherine's wheel turns'. Then, upon leaving, 'she's got her Catherine wheels on'.

The song is composed of two distinct sections. The first, in E minor, focuses on the discontent in the relationship and the notion Catherine has about leaving. Hester is on the brushes again and there are lovely contributions from mandolin and piano to compliment the acoustic guitar. By the 2:20 mark, it sounds like the song is coming to an end as the band enter one of their distinctive codas. The second section, starting at 3:00, is in D major, with a more uplifting feeling now that Catherine has left: 'She's gone, vanished in the night'. Seymour turns his plain bass line into another groovy Motown line and the section comes alive. Again, like in 'Walking On The Spot', by using a rising melody, Finn creates the optimistic sense of release Catherine is hoping for, even on the line: 'Bruises come up dark'. During the short instrumental break between verses, there is the unusual vocal choice of 'ba-bomp-ba-bom-bom…' low in the mix – the guys are still having fun in the studio.

Considering Crowded House's general adherence to concise, compact songs, 'Catherine Wheels' is, by comparison, quite adventurous, with two distinct movements telling two parts of the story. Still, it's all tied together nicely by Finn's continuous guitar strumming for the full 5:12.

'Skin Feeling' (Paul Hester)

Never let it be said that Crowded House are not a rock band. Despite being known for their acoustic sound, sensitive lyrics and velvety vocals, every album released to this point has had at least one song that amps up the guitars and drums: 'Love You 'Til The Day I Die', 'Kill Eye', 'Fame Is'. This one has two in the form of 'Locked Out' and 'Skin Feeling'. With the latter – Hester's contribution to *Together Alone* – the Crowdies, as Hester liked to refer to the band, went full-on *Achtung Baby*-era U2.

There can be no greater happiness than one that has risen from the ashes of despair. Hester, sounding not unlike Finn here, sings about a joy so great that he feels reborn: 'My second life has just begun with this hungry girl'. He has found delight in the small things that make up a life: 'I like the smell of that shop … I like the kids when they're asleep … I like the people on TV'. At the apex of this happiness pyramid is the woman he loves: 'I love the pigment in your skin, I love the way it moves me'. She has helped him to feel younger and better about himself. After what Finn wrote about in 'Black And White Boy', he must have been thrilled to see Hester waxing poetic about a love strong enough to maintain life.

Mark Hart provides spoken vocals – phased and distorted like Bono on 'The Fly' – that detail other things this narrator might like. 'Skin Feeling' is at once a pastiche, a tribute and a fresh take, all of which Crowded House, the rockers, pull off with ease.

'Together Alone' (Neil Finn/Bub Wehi/Mark Hart)

Neil Finn talked about 'Together Alone' in a documentary on the making of the album in 1993:

> It was an idea that came about during the recording of the album that we should try and write something to draw in what we saw as a few strands of New Zealand music. Obviously, a Māori singing group was a pretty central part of the New Zealand experience. Brass bands used to play on the back of trucks at Christmas time; it was a sound I loved. And the log drummers were something I'd become aware of only during that period, although it's as old as the hills. We thought we'd unite them all. I wrote a song based on that idea. We got together with Bub Wehi from the Te Whakatohea Māori group in west Auckland and he wrote the Māori lyrics. So, really, it was well conceived and, I think, a beautiful end to the record. It was a fantastic day. We had microphones across the valley that were recording ambient things. They picked up very loud crickets. At some point during the end of the song, the crickets get very much in sync with the log drummers, which is wonderful and magical.

The biculturalism of New Zealand has nurtured artists like Crowded House to include and share the elements of Māori culture in their music. In the context of *Together Alone*, this all sounds like the most natural thing to do. There is an earthiness to the Crowded House sound – perhaps more on this album than any other – a sense that it has been created organically, blossoming out of the environment as a result.

'Together Alone' is a song about that unique relationship. Finn's lyric speaks of unity among communities: 'I'm still your friend when you are in need. As is once will always be. Earth and sky. Moon and sea'. Bub Wehi, a musical and cultural Kiwi icon, translated the sentiment into *te reo Māori:* 'Rangi the sky-father is above. The earth mother is below. Our love for one another is everlasting'.

Mid-song, we hear a Karanga, the traditional Māori call of welcome. As the singers finish, the horns and other instruments fade, leaving only the sound of log drums. At their sudden conclusion, the last sound on the album is of a joyous celebration from everyone present.

Recurring Dream: The Very Best Of Crowded House (1996)

Personnel on the three new songs:
Neil Finn: guitar, keyboards, lead and backing vocals
Nick Seymour: bass, backing vocals
Paul Hester: drums
Mark Hart: guitar, keyboards, backing vocals
Producer: Mitchell Froom, Tchad Blake, Neil Finn
Engineer: Tchad Blake
Assistant Engineers: Andrew Buckton, Nick Abbott
Recorded in 1996 in York Street Studios (Auckland, NZ)
Released in June 1996 on Capitol Records
Three new songs written by Neil Finn
Running Order: 'Weather With You', 'World Where You Live', 'Fall At Your Feet', 'Locked Out', 'Don't Dream It's Over', 'Into Temptation', 'Pineapple Head', 'When You Come', 'Private Universe', 'Not The Girl You Think You Are', 'Instinct', 'I Feel Possessed', 'Four Seasons In One Day', 'It's Only Natural', 'Distant Sun', 'Something So Strong', 'Mean To Me', 'Better Be Home Soon', 'Everything Is Good For You'

In the same year that Crowded House announced their dissolution (premature as it may have been) – capping it off with a stellar farewell concert in the forecourt of Sydney's iconic opera house – they released this compilation.

As was the trend in the 1980s and 1990s, this greatest hits compilation includes three unreleased songs. They were positioned, of course, as an incentive to buy the album, which contains 16 previously released songs – four from each album – and to use as singles to promote the collection. The irony is that they appeared on a 'Best Of' without anyone actually having heard them. Typically, with some exceptions, new songs released on a compilation would not perform as well on the charts or even among the artist's fans. The three new songs on *Recurring Dream* are no different.

'Not The Girl You Think You Are', 'Instinct' and 'Everything Is Good For You' are fine songs. Had they been created by a lesser songwriter than Neil Finn, they could be categorised as quite good. But, in the context of Crowded House, they are inferior, which makes the irony of them being included on this compilation even greater (although 'Everything Is Good For You' did manage to climb to number ten on the Australian singles chart in 1996). It isn't difficult to figure out why: Crowded House were, at the time of this release, officially broken up.

Finn had been asked to contribute three new songs for the compilation by Capitol Records, which he did willingly. They even brought Paul Hester back into the studio to play drums and reunited with Mitchell Froom and Tchad Blake. But the results suggest Finn's heart wasn't really in it. It suggests a mid-career lull, especially knowing that the Finn Brothers had just released *Finn* – their first album as a duo – and that Neil was getting ready to record his first solo album *Try Whistling This*. In this context, Finn might have been saving his better songs for the other projects. The three new songs are dynamically flat and melodically unadventurous. They sound very much unlike Crowded House, each one desperately crying out for a hooky chorus or sneaky chord change. In the 2023 Zoom conversation, Finn elaborated:

> At that point, I decided to break the band up. But we got back together in the studio to do those three songs with Tchad and Mitchell and Paul, the old team, so they became Crowded House songs. I guess I would have recorded them in some other fashion had we not done that. They are Crowded House tracks because they were recorded by Crowded House. I don't necessarily sit down and specify what I'm writing for. It becomes that because the band get a hold of it.

The other factor dulling the lustre of the new songs is that the first two were sandwiched between 16 of Crowded House's legitimate best. When placed between the masterfully atmospheric 'Private Universe' and the enchanting 'I Feel Possessed', the odds were against any new song. The third debutante is tacked on at the end.

Having said this, *Recurring Dream* did capture the ARIA in 1997 as the highest-selling album of the year in Australia, outselling Jimmy Barnes, John Farnham, Powderfinger and the monstrous debut by Savage Garden.

Recurring Dream is named after a song in the Crowded House tool bag. Written during the Mullanes era, it endured many evolutionary changes before finally being released in its full form as a B-side to 'Instinct' in 1996 and then on *Afterglow*.

'Not The Girl You Think You Are'

A simple song about self-deception, the obvious implication of the lyric – 'They're not his shoes under your bed' – is that she is deceiving her man. But the fine print offers a different take: she is being deceived and, even worse, is deceiving herself. She believes she's living a life of privilege where she is treated like a princess. This man is using her as a beard of some kind, a trophy companion. He doesn't care who's riding in the car next to him 'with the top down and the wind blowing … He won't deceive you or tell you the truth … He won't write you letters'. He doesn't have to go out of his way to please her because she's already convinced herself that she's special. If she believes that, he's done his job. As the song nears its end, she is again fooled by being told, 'Believe you have one', which is actually, 'Believe you have won'.

There is a dark, film noir tone to the song, played in a slow waltz. Out of the three new singles, it was the third single release. The arrangement, framed around an acoustic guitar and a second-hand electric keyboard called an Optigan, never really gets going. Uncharacteristically, it mainly stays at one disappointing dynamic from beginning to end, diluting an otherwise decent melody.

Finn's double-tracked lead vocals – here sounding not unlike Badly Drawn Boy's Damon Gough – give the narrative an extra frisson as if the woman is being watched from all angles. Notably, Finn does not use any first-person pronouns in this song; there are only mentions of 'You' and 'He', with the suggestion that 'I' might be an uncredited third wheel.

'Instinct'

Assuming Neil Finn set out early on to create memorable songs that made heavy use of vertical melodies with the occasional soaring singalong chorus, a case could be made that he wasn't trying at all with 'Instinct'. His melody in this song is the most horizontal of any Crowded House composition to date, staying virtually on one note for ten full bars of the verse until finally moving on, using his falsetto, in the chorus – 'When your turn comes round…' – sounding much more like himself. It doesn't help that there is little harmonic movement underneath. It simply doesn't meet the high bar set by the first four Crowded House albums. There's little evidence to believe it would have made the cut for any of those, let alone this compilation.

Having said that, 'Instinct' could have been in the repertoire of any number of bands in the late 1980s, like Icehouse, The Fixx or Howard Jones. It's just not very Crowded House-y. Highlights include a terrific Seymour bass line and Finn's vocal performance. It was the first single released in the UK and the second elsewhere.

It's a song about a transition of sorts: 'Felt the burden lifting from my back', 'Separate the fiction from the fact … but it's nearly time to flick the switch'. Our narrator has taken strides to change the status quo – 'I lit the match' – after a long stretch of letting things slide. Ultimately, he seems pretty pleased with his decision, owing it all to acting on impulse and gut instinct. What he's changing exactly is unclear, and maybe it doesn't matter.

'Everything Is Good For You'

This is Finn's take on the famous Friedrich Nietzsche aphorism, 'What does not kill me makes me stronger'. It's something many of us have been told by a caring friend during a period of struggle. There is some truth in it; however, it shouldn't take a near-death experience to strengthen one's resilience.

Here, Finn focuses on the random connections we make with people and our ability to find meaning in this randomness. The first verse sees an angry protester meeting a woman equally determined to overcome a great sadness: 'All paths lead to a single conclusion'. The second verse focuses on people living on the edge, exploring high-risk activities that they hope will set them free. Finn posits in the chorus that these nourishing events will make you stronger. He also suggests that we should accept these transitional times, even if it means capitalising on another's misfortune: 'One man's ending is another man's beginning'.

Clearly, Finn was in a different zone during the writing of these songs because, like 'Instinct', the melody of 'Everything Is Good For You' is equally as horizontal. The repetition in the verse melody actually gets tiring. Continuing the Lennon and McCartney comparison, this sounds as if it could be one of Lennon's melodies, if perhaps a bit poppier in feel. It's like 'Gimme Some Truth' seen through rose-coloured glasses. That is until it gets to the bridge, where it suddenly sounds very much like Crowded House indeed. The melody slows down as it winds its way through the chords, the voices in harmony reminiscent of Neil and Tim on *Woodface*.

Of the three new songs on *Recurring Dream*, this is the strongest. Seymour's bassline grooves with an almost psychedelic lilt and Hart plays a steady guitar arpeggio throughout that holds the whole arrangement together. There is some satisfying electric guitar as the song fades out. As a greatest hits inclusion, it could have gotten away with opening the album rather than closing it. As a finale, it's a bit of a let-down.

Afterglow (1999)

An enthusiastic fan of any artist would certainly be excited to learn that a collection of rarities and outtakes – songs that didn't make the cut for any album – would be released. A listener – whose collection was incomplete without absolutely everything their favourite band recorded – might even stand in line in the rain to wait for their local HMV to open so they could be the first to purchase the long-awaited recordings. Thankfully, those days are gone – with rare exceptions, it was usually not worth the wait.

Having said that, most of *Afterglow* sounds like it could be a complete Crowded House album. Of the 13 songs on the original 1999 release, eight of them are strong enough to have been considered for inclusion on any of the four albums released to date. 'Private Universe' is a new mix of the great song released on *Together Alone* and the other three could have been left off without any complaints. So, nearly 70% of *Afterglow* is worth listening to. For fans saddened by their breakup and having waited three years since *Recurring Dream* and six years from the last complete album of original material, *Afterglow* would have been a dream come true. Finn reflected on this release during the 2023 Zoom conversation:

> I can't honestly remember the songs we put on there. There would have been flaws in them – I'd never resolved a lyric or something else that would have stopped them from making their way onto albums. We had too many songs anyway, so something had to give. I like the alternative version of 'Private Universe' without all the slightly electronic aspects to it, which was fun at the time, but it didn't seem overly 'us'.

Production credits are listed with each song. Musical personnel would correspond with the band line-up at the time of recording.

'I Am In Love' (Neil Finn)
Produced by Youth and Crowded House
Recorded at Karekare by Greg Hunter in 1992
Originally released on the 'Private Universe' CD single in 1994
Recorded during the *Together Alone* sessions, 'I Am In Love' is a strong enough song to have made it onto that album, but there are some key points in the music and lyrics to suggest why it didn't.

As far as Neil Finn is concerned, this song lacks some of the craftier wordplay and density of narrative as many of his other Crowded House songs. Not that there is anything wrong with a straightforward love song. In fact, what's unique about this lyric is how it doesn't put the object of the singer's love on a pedestal. Rather, it focuses on the mystery of falling in love, specifically how one might act foolishly in a blind effort to show their love and still be amazed when they find they are loved in return: 'These things that I have done, they would be a test of anyone'. It's less 'Why you?' and more 'Why me?' But later on, the narrator's reflection on the theory that we end up marrying versions of our parents is a weird distraction and perhaps more relevant in a conversation with a therapist.

Still, he states plainly, 'I am in love', several times. This alone cannot be questioned. But, as Finn explained to Radio New Zealand's Jeremy Ansell:

> Perhaps I was a little sheepish bout the title being so direct, but there is no particular reason why it didn't make *Together Alone*.

Overall, the musicianship and melody are strong. The verses, sung over rumbling drums and a steady bass pedal (staying on the same root note), are in the key of B Mixolydian, which means the seventh note of the scale is flattened. This gives the verses a mystical, tribal sound. Then, as Finn sings 'I am in…' on the flattened seventh at the beginning of the chorus, he creates a more bluesy sound that resolves satisfyingly on the E major.

An early demo reveals a more traditional Nick Seymour bass line, one that previous producer Mitchell Froom might have elicited. It's a straightforward Motown groove that would have sounded at home on any previous Crowded House album. Producer Youth, on the other hand, heard a more sparse, atmospheric arrangement with heavy use of toms and less busy bass.

'Sacred Cow' (Neil Finn)

Produced by Mitchell Froom
Recorded and mixed at A&M Studios by Tchad Blake in 1990

Recorded early on during the *Woodface* sessions, 'Sacred Cow' probably missed the cut because it sounded too similar to other Crowded House songs. The guitar work is a combination of 'Now We're Getting Somewhere' and 'Love This Life', and the overall feel has a bit of 'Sister Madly' to it.

This is another lyric heavily weighted down with fallout from Finn's religious upbringing. It's one thing to state that he won't suffer fools gladly; it's quite another, as he does here, to root those fools in a morass of religious rhetoric and man-made symbolism, although he seems to admit it's not an easy position to be in. There are confusing and sometimes contradictory perspectives here. The narrator seems to have been misled early on – 'You got me going,' 'You let me down again' – but, nevertheless, refuses to get sucked into his persecutor's orbit: 'You're not mysterious now, I don't worship that sacred cow'. Further on, he then acknowledges, 'You know what's good for me', suggesting the narrator's difficulty in entirely abandoning his religion.

Finn admits it's a disjointed song. Not for the first time, producer Froom suggested combining elements of two or more different songs to create a new one. In the Deluxe Edition in 2016, Finn was quoted as saying:

> This was one of the first songs we recorded, and I think it was a very worthy song. Some of them worked out. This one now sounds good to me.

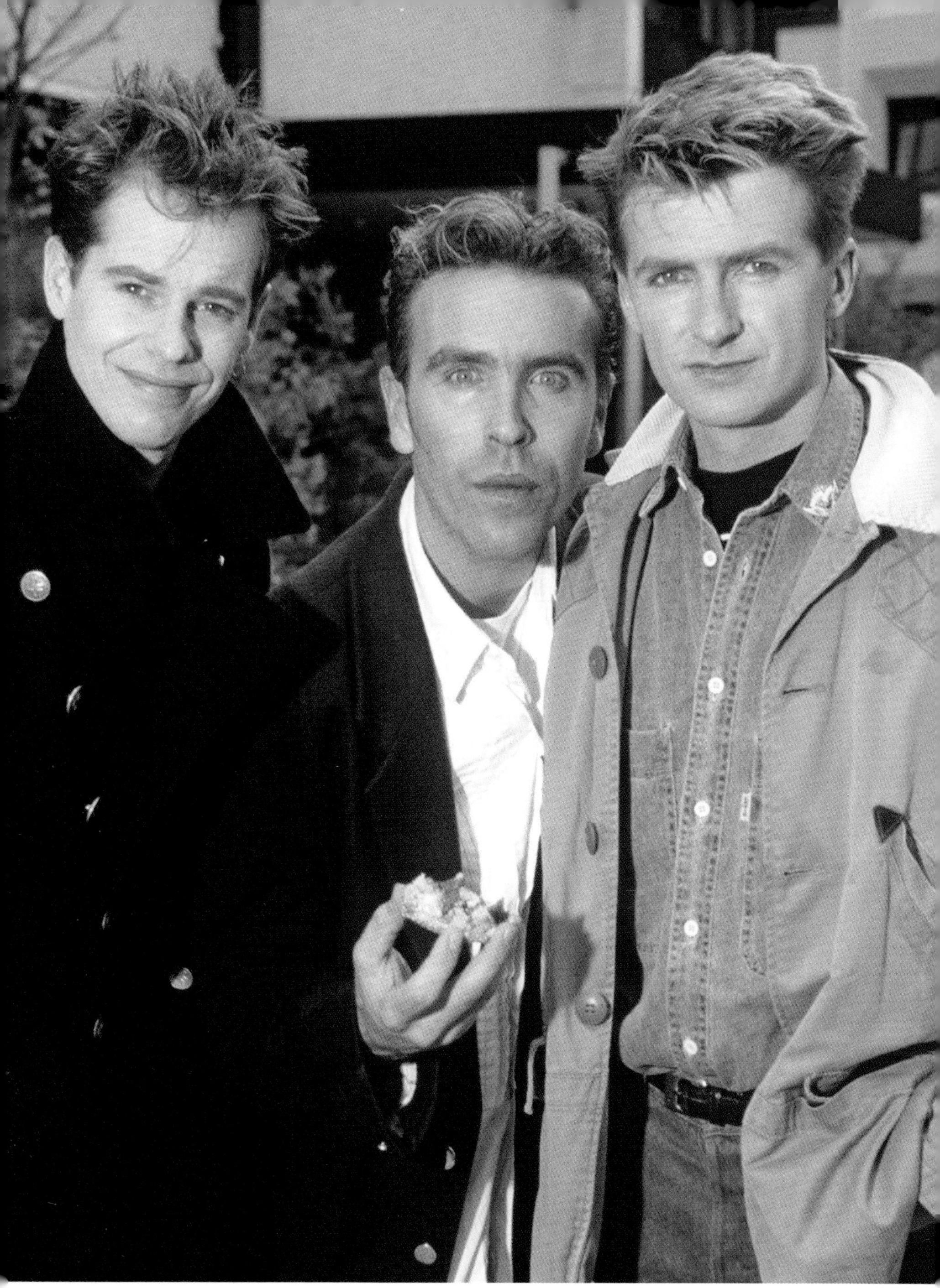

Above: Stepping out, Crowded House in the early days. Paul Hester, Nick Seymour and Neil Finn. (*Alamy*)

Left: *Crowded House*: 'It was a way of capturing something about each personality'. (*Capitol Records*)

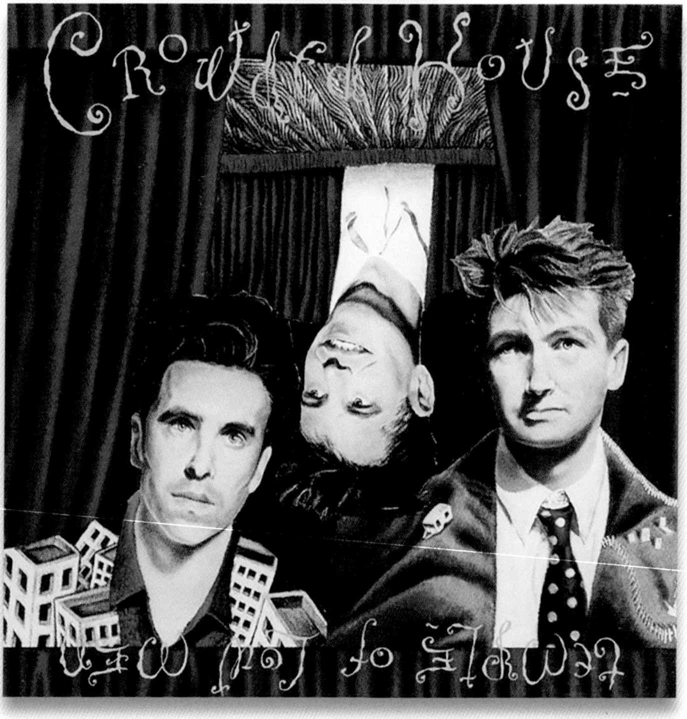

Right: *Temple Of Low Men*: 'Crumbling under the power of some higher power'. (*Capitol Records*)

Right: *Woodface*: 'Look, there it is … so simple and obvious'. (*Capitol Records*)

Left: *Together Alone*: 'I made the mistake of painting a likeness of Muhammad'. (*Capitol Records*)

Above: Walking on the pier. The Mullanes in the brief period between Split Enz and Crowded House: Seymour, Finn, Craig Hooper and Hester. (*neilfinn.com*)

Left: The band wearing Seymour's original hand-painted stage outfits, 1988. (*Lynn Goldsmith, The Guardian*)

Above: A baby-faced band enjoying the company of Tim Finn during his short but productive stay in Crowded House, 1991. (*neilfinn.com*)
Below: Hart, Hester, Finn and Seymour on Karekare Beach, New Zealand during the recording of *Together Alone*, 1993. (*neilfinn.com*)

Left and below: Telling the story of Crowded House in the video for 'Don't Dream It's Over'.

Left and top right over page: At the seaside for the 'Weather With You' video.

Left and below: Darkness and light in the video for 'Distant Sun', 1993.

Left: *Time On Earth*: 'It was spawned by my concern for Paul.' (*BMG*)

Right: *Intriguer*: 'I wanted to show something that was quite childlike.' (*BMG*)

Right: *Dreamers Are Waiting*. 'It's just the right size'. (*EMI*)

Left: *Gravity Stairs*. A departure from the colourful covers to a more monochromatic palette. (*BMG*)

Above: Drummerless and rudderless, Hart, Finn and Seymour are pictured here around the release of *Recurring Dream*, 1996. (*neilfinn.com*)
Below: A rare band shot with drummer Peter Jones in 1999 after Hester's departure. (*Patrick Ford/Redferns*)

Above and left:
Saying farewell to the world at the Sydney Opera House, 1996 (*neilfinn.com*)

Above: Reuniting for *Time On Earth* with drummer Matt Sherrod, 2007. (*neilfinn.com*)

Below: Crowded House mark III: Seymour, Finn the Elder and Finns the Younger flocking Froom the veteran rookie, 2021. (*Kerry Brown, The Guardian*)

Right: Liam Finn goes full Pete Townsend, Crowded House on stage 2022. (*neilfinn.com*)

Below: 'Don't Dream It's Over' live off the floor in three continents during the COVID lockdown, 2020.

Left: 'Don't Stop Now' video, 2007. 'Sometimes you have to turn the wrong way 'round'.

Right: From the 'Saturday Sun' video in 2010. 'The game is still on'.

Left: Back in the frame. The video for 'To The Island', 2021.

Right: 'Never seen such a thing.' 'Playing With Fire' video, 2021.

Left: A proud Papa on the Pyramid Stage at Glastonbury Festival, 2022. (*YouTube*)

Right: Finn the elder in the video for 'Teenage Summer', 2024.

Right: *Recurring Dream*. Beyond the dreamlike into nightmare territory. (*Capitol Records*)

Left: *Afterglow*: 'It's just ideas thrown together with a deadline.' (*Capitol Records*)

> At the time, I think, I was a little bit unsure of whether the lyrics resolved themselves. In fact, I had no idea what the hell the song meant.

'Sacred Cow's verses were largely taken from a demo called 'You Got Me Going' and its chorus from an early song called 'Cigarette Girl'. Apparently, the guitar intro was originally heard on one of Finn's homemade four-track demos in an instrumental called 'Sax Boogie'. It's an enjoyable listen that includes horns and excellent guitar playing.

'You Can Touch' (Neil Finn)
Produced by Youth and Crowded House
Recorded at Karekare by Greg Hunter in 1992
Originally released on the UK CD single for 'Nails In My Feet' in 1993
One of the standout melodies on *Afterglow*, 'You Can Touch' could very easily have appeared on *Together Alone*. The tight harmonies also have a strong Finn Brothers/*Woodface* feeling to them. What makes this melody so appealing is that we never quite know where it's going to go next. The opening line – 'It could spell…' – quickly uses the minor seventh and sixth notes of the Bb minor chord, leaving a suspended pause that keeps listeners hanging before resolving – '…my near defeat' – on the major seventh, which also happens to be the third (mediant) of the F major chord that follows, firmly embedding it in that chord. This repeats for the second line before an unexpected shift to Bb major with an equally major-based melody: 'And tears will fall and oceans will rise', which includes a descending harmony with the ascending melody.

We then come to what counts as the chorus: 'And you can touch me, I won't hide'. It's back to the Bb major to F major change before a shift to the F minor7 chord. Finn's melody stays on the F during this change, creating a smooth transition marked by the harmony that moves with the chord.

Some great guitar work from both Finn and Hart fills this song out after the second chorus and again at the fade out. We hear another version of the Māori strum, this time with some distortion and a guitar soloing over the top of it. The chorus section includes one of Seymour's more memorable bass lines.

Drums stay out of the arrangement until the second verse. There's a story behind this, which Finn recounted during the 2023 Zoom conversation:

> 'You Can Touch' is a song that would have made the album, but we never got a good drum track for it. Paul got really pissed off about it one night and went down to the accommodation. He couldn't quite get it. And then I got on the drum kit and did about seven drum tracks in a row. We used them all. We did a couple of tracks of drums and gave them to Bob Clearmountain to mix. It was just this big caterwauling drum mess, which we didn't put on *Afterglow*. He said, 'Neil, I really like your songs and your

voice and I love mixing your stuff, but I can't mix this. The drums are too messy and just bad.'

The simple lyric is told from the perspective of someone down on his luck, encountered by another person who stands to gain by offering help. The simple act of laying on hands might, in this scenario, bring solace to both the afflicted and the deliverer. It's a win-win situation. Nobody is asking for a miracle, just a simple touch.

'Help Is Coming' (Neil Finn, Peter Jones)
Produced by Crowded House
Recorded at York Street Studios by Nick Abbott and Andrew Buckton in 1994
Ellis Island sits in New York harbour and, starting in the late 19th century, was used as a processing facility for European immigrants to the United States. Up until World War II, it was the primary first stop for people looking to America for a safe haven and quickly became a symbol of their doorway to freedom.

Finn sings, in short, succinct lines, about people on ships desperate for help. It can't be made any starker than 'Help is coming'. The second verse suggests that these immigrants – like Finn's mother emigrating from Ireland – are actually on their way to Australia/New Zealand because he uses the images of 'Distant drummin'' – suggesting the sounds of traditional Māori drums – and 'Lyrebirds callin'', a bird found exclusively in Australia and whose image is used on coins, stamps and crests. If this is the case, when Finn sings, 'We sail tomorrow for Ellis Island', it is simply used symbolically as a place people strive to reach to 'Escape the anguish of our past and pray'. It's a song about unbridled hope despite the prospect of an unknown future: 'Dreams come true', Finn sings plainly. Notably, some 20 years after it was recorded, 'Help Is Coming' was used in a fundraising campaign by Save the Children's Refugee Crisis Appeal to aid in the Syrian refugee relief effort.

The slinky arrangement has an atmosphere that would be appropriate for the *Together Alone* album: well-fitted steel guitar and a very Youth-inspired minimalist approach.

One of four songs recorded in 1995 at what ended up being the last recording session before Crowded House broke up, 'Help Is Coming' included the contribution of drummer Peter Jones, who stepped into the drum chair toward the end of the *Together Alone* tour after Hester decided to leave. His addition is defined by Seymour on Neil Finn's website:

> We developed a rhythm section relationship that felt very comfortable to me. It was probably more groove-based than song-based when we were arranging things in pre-production. 'Help Is Coming' definitely had a very groove-oriented aspiration. He was a soul and jazz drummer.

Never underestimate the power of the rhythm section. The groove in 'Help Is Coming' is slow and deliberate but definitely groovy. Jones toured and recorded with the band for two years, returning briefly as part of the *Farewell To The World* concert in Sydney in 1996. He became a full-time teacher and died in 2012.

'I Love You Dawn' (Neil Finn)
Produced by Crowded House
Recorded at Platinum Studios by Chris Corr circa 1989
Aside from the beautiful sentiment of this love song, it's very forgettable. The melody in the A section is catchy – like a children's song – but, overall, quite dull. In the B section, Finn employs a more interesting melody using chromatic intervals up and down the scale and incorporates some delicious harmonies, but ultimately, it doesn't go anywhere. Whereas a majority of Finn's songs throw in a surprising chord change, unexpected melodic movements, a beautiful bridge or chorus and lyrics sharp enough to slice off a pineapple head, this song has practically none of these things. For a songwriter of his calibre, this is striking and leaves little doubt as to why it never made it onto one of the band's major releases.

Originally intended for the *Woodface* album, this demo for 'I Love You Dawn' got separated from the flock after Tim Finn came into the fray and the brothers began co-writing for the album in earnest. As Finn elaborated in the 2016 Deluxe Edition:

> The problem with a lot of those original demos is that there was just too much good stuff around and they were kind of old and so we'd kind of grown out of them. But this was always, in my mind, a really worthy demo, a good performance and it's kind of special because it's a song I wrote for my wife, Sharon Dawn, and it's quite a direct song for me.

The most telling lyric – 'Above the billboards and the hordes, magazines and rock awards, we can't afford to pay our bills' – shows that outside the charm and glamour of being an internationally known musician, he and his wife would be just as concerned with their day-to-day obligations as any other couple. It also shows that despite his success, there is no excess, something that might be a source of pride.

'Dr. Livingston' (Neil Finn)
Produced by Crowded House
Recorded at Platinum Studios by Chris Corr circa 1989
Originally released on the UK CD single 'Four Seasons In One Day' in 1992
This is an atypically political song for Finn, who wrote it after a visit to Mozambique. There isn't much in the way of a narrative in this song; rather, it's a series of highlights from what he might have seen, heard or learned

about the country. 'Steam ship sail down the river, fight the mosquitoes that lie in the swamp', Finn sings. This is the kind of imagery that pigeonholed many African countries as backward or savage to the colonisers. When the real Dr David Livingstone (with an 'e'), the Scottish explorer and missionary, led several expeditions into Africa, they were largely failures – 'See Dr Livingston land with a thump'. He was unable to secure the trade deals Britain desired, but he still represents a time when colonial Britain was an empire to be feared and respected.

However, it doesn't quite rise to the challenge of honouring Mozambique. It could be the amount of sadness in the lyrics, with the mention of 'sad willows', 'dying babies' and 'under the gun'. There is a standout reference to the region being conquered to the utter enjoyment of the conquerors: 'Blow up the bridges and come like a storm'. The song really gets lost when Finn sings, 'I am a white man in Africa'. His melody is appropriately eerie, but actually, the sentiment comes off as something all the more uncomfortable.

Recorded in a steady 6/8 shuffle during a session between the releases of *Temple Of Low Men* and *Woodface*, 'Dr Livingston' is catchy with a strong chorus. 'I hear the drums, I know it's urgent, I hear survival in his hands'. In the outro, Finn screams extemporaneously in a monotone (similar to 'Whispers And Moans') to great effect: 'Hours later the thought of my bed makes me tired and ready for sleep'. The playing is strong, including some really solid, in-the-pocket drumming from Hester.

'My Telly's Gone Bung' (Paul Hester)
Produced by Crowded House
Recorded at Platinum Studios by Chris Corr circa 1989
There isn't much mystery to this song, but it's classic Paul Hester. His enthralling sense of humour and joie de vivre are in every line. Had it not been for 'Italian Plastic' – Hester's other song recorded during the same sessions – it might have made it onto *Woodface*.

According to Finn, Hester was a notorious television addict. With cheeky references to 'the ABC' (Australian Broadcasting Corporation) and 'Kylie & Jason' (Minogue and Donovan, stars of the hit Australian soap opera *Neighbours*, who had an on-and-off-screen relationship), it bounces along like a sitcom theme song, aided by the plunky piano solo.

Hester's refrain – 'I've waited up for you to come alive and bring some truth back to me' – is probably the most serious lyric in the song. One can imagine him sitting in front of a screen plastered with static, waiting for the return of his favourite show, something that would make someone with bipolar disorder absolutely furious or, conversely, in a state of zen. In this case, it sounds like the latter: 'I'm where I wanna be, in front of my TV'.

It's not a classic Crowded House song. Still, it ends on a rather joyous note as the repeated 'If it was up to me' – sounding very much like the ending of Three Dog Night's 'Mama Told Me (Not To Come)' – suggests he is relinquishing control of the situation and will simply wait until normal programming resumes.

'Private Universe' (Zen Mix) (Neil Finn)
Produced by Youth and Crowded House
Recorded at Karekare by Greg Hunter in 1992
This stripped-down version reduces the *Together Alone* standout to two acoustic guitar tracks, lead vocal, sparse harmonies and lots of reverb. With the most noticeable change being the absence of log drummers, this version capitalises on Finn's excellent vocal performance and captures the intimacy inherent to the song's theme.

Finn admitted in the 2023 Zoom conversation that this was one of his favourite Crowded House songs.

'Lester' (Neil Finn)
Produced by Crowded House
Recorded by Nel Finn at his home studio in 1988
In the music videos for 'Weather With You' and 'Everything Is Good For You', there are passing glimpses of a Dalmatian frolicking with the members of Crowded House, his black and white spots starkly monochrome against the band members' customary colourful garb. That's Lester, Neil Finn's dog – the aforementioned black-and-white boy.

It's a transformative song of sorts, using the trope of 'I will change if...', often seen in movies where the bullish protagonist succumbs to prayer while a loved one's life hangs in the balance. Here, Finn promises – to nobody but himself, perhaps – to alter his behaviour after his dog is nearly killed in the street after being hit by a car. So he sings, 'I will change if Lester lives', but doesn't promise to be a better person overall; he simply vows to be a better dog owner, to 'not mess him 'round just 'cause I own him'.

The verse melody starts in a minor key as strong as most Crowded House songs. However, by the end of the verse, it sounds as if Finn has run out of ideas ('The screeching tyres never seem to end'). Overall, the lyric is plodding and plain and, by Finn's standards, doesn't rise to his own high bar. Naturally, the chorus shifts to a major key as Finn sings his promises, but here, too, the melody doesn't go anywhere. It seems to drift off as if Finn hasn't fully finished his thoughts.

For all this, it should be noted that this is the only one of Finn's home demos that made it to a major release. The recording is intimate and crisp, with two acoustic guitar tracks, a bit of lead guitar at the end, a lead vocal and two or three backing vocal tracks. The only indication of it being a home recording is a nearly imperceptible puff into the microphone as Finn sings the 'he' of 'he had good luck and strong bones' at 0:50.

'Anyone Can Tell' (Neil Finn)
Produced by Mitchell Froom and Crowded House
Recorded at A&M Studios by Tchad Blake in 1989
Originally released on the UK CD single for 'Chocolate Cake' in 1991
Another great Neil Finn melody that got lost in the forest of great Neil Finn melodies. Recorded for *Woodface*, 'Anyone Can Tell' could have held fast with any of the songs on that album. However, it was ultimately let down by an ineffective arrangement that didn't meet the high bar set by the other songs.

The singer shares images from his dreams: 'a place that's hedged with roses' and 'a place that's overrun by children'. Yet, it remains unclear what the rest of those dreams are supposed to mean. The lyric is scattered with obscure and seemingly unrelated comments: 'The truth is still a valuable thing. Don't get caught with your pants down, baby'.

The song is held up by a catchy chorus and the first instance of backing vocals occurring in the call-and-response chanting of the title line. But still, lyrically, there is no straight line: 'Anyone can tell that I'm not lying', he sings. Lying about what exactly? Getting caught with your pants down? The second half of the chorus then seems to contradict the first half: 'You can hide your face, pull it into shapes. But you can't escape the lie forever'. So, who's lying now? It's like a confusing soap opera plot.

Despite the typically excellent musicianship, particularly Seymour's invigorating bass line in the verses, the overall arrangement is missing the band's signature sonic dynamics. The guitars are thin and sound like a first-take idea. A mysterious harmonica blows twice in the introduction, only to remain unheard for the rest of the song. Starting at 2:40, during the guitar solo outro, an odd-sounding string pad lingers below the band, leading the song towards a more psychedelic ending.

Overall, 'Anyone Can Tell' is an enjoyable listen and stands out as one of the highlights of *Afterglow*.

'Recurring Dream' (Neil Finn, Paul Hester, Nick Seymour and Craig Hooper)
Produced by Crowded House
Recorded at Platinum Studios in 1985
Original version released as a B-side to 'Now We're Getting Somewhere' in 1986
Full version originally heard on the soundtrack to the film Tequila Sunrise in 1988, then with the UK CD single for 'Instinct' in 1996
It's no wonder this song sounds like Split Enz era Neil Finn because it goes way back to the period between that band and Crowded House. During the short-lived tenure of The Mullanes, 'Recurring Dream' started as an instrumental and evolved into a B-side release with only one verse before maturing into the version that appears on *Afterglow*. Notably, the song did not appear on the 1996 greatest hits package *Recurring Dream*.

This lyric again shows Finn's unique talent for finding new perspectives on old themes. Whereas a recurring dream may appear mysterious, even nightmarish, Finn's 'Recurring Dream' is welcomed as a template for all things sweet and wonderful – a rebirth of sorts. He sings about the complex world in his mind where 'there are a million things spilling over'. Yet, in his dream – which might actually be reality – he is touched by a 'warm wind' and he sees his 'windows wiping clean'. Everything is becoming clear and manageable, reminding him of his good fortune. He is undeniably happy in this song. The word 'dream' is, in this case, used in the rhetorical sense to indicate having reached a place of long-imagined perfection.

The arrangement's four-on-the-floor drive and 'Can't Carry On' tempo add to the uplifting spirit of the song, while the melody in the chorus – dropping vertically over the minor chord changes – gives the sense of wanting to go on forever. The chorus resolves satisfyingly as Finn sings, 'It's my recurring dream', over the tonic of G major – all grounded and strong.

Finn's talents as a guitarist – often overlooked in the face of his other abilities – are on show here. The song opens with a busy, semiquaver (sixteenth notes) guitar riff that is maintained throughout. It's part country picking (in fact, part of the original instrumental version of 'Recurring Dream' was called 'Hoedown') and part King Crimson. That Finn is able to sing while simultaneously playing the riff, as proven in a live video, is a testament to his talents.

'Left Hand' (Neil Finn)
Produced by Crowded House
Recorded at Periscope Studios by Paul Kosky in 1990
Arguably one of the most uncharacteristic grooves ever created by Crowded House, this is a slow, blues-funk (or funk-blues) song very much in the style of Joe Cocker's 'You Can Leave Your Hat On' (written by Randy Newman). Chugging piano chord quavers (eighth notes), a snaking bass line, wah-wah guitar and bluesy vocals characterise this track.

Finn commented on this during the 2023 Zoom conversation:

> We had a potential funk element and Nick always wanted to be in a funk band. On his first demo, he sent in a bass line for 'That's What I Call Love', which was completely different from anything I'd ever worked with before and it got him the job. So, we never truly went in that direction, but we had it lurking.

The chorus of 'Left Hand' had gone through many incarnations, matched up with an unsuitable verse on a Mullanes song and another unusual pairing with one of Hester's songs during Crowded House's early days.

The lyric is short and simple. In this narrative, Finn sings about a relationship where each participant represents one equal half. If one half isn't pulling their weight, the other half is surely obliged to point it out. One member of the couple is the left hand and the other is the right. They must act as one person in order to put their hands together – in prayer, in applause or to keep warm. That they don't communicate well is not in question: 'You pick me up and then you put me down', the narrator sings. What seems to be unclear is what either of them wants to do about it.

The verses – in which Finn outlines the ways in which this couple call each other out – use the occasional bar of 2/4 – out of the basic 4/4 groove – to illustrate their out-of-sync communication. As the audience trip over this stutter step, surely, too, does the couple. 'It was typical of you', he sings by way of denying responsibility. 'There is nowhere to go, I'm not hanging around'. Clearly, he wants out and wants to let go of the other hand. Still, he can't stop referring to their hands – her on the left, him on the right or vice versa – admitting that perhaps they are one after all.

'Time Immemorial' (Neil Finn)
Produced by Crowded House
Recorded at Platinum Studios by Chris Corr circa 1989
Another *Woodface* outtake, 'Time Immemorial' is crafted from the same template as 'Kill Eye', 'Mansion In The Slums', 'There Goes God' and 'Fame Is' – it's another attempt to make sense of how money, fame and power have tainted organised religion. In this case, Finn focuses on the reasons believers ask for God's help and the dubious ways that is done.

Verse one asks the question: Can you make a decision and take responsibility for it afterwards? Verse two points out, 'The house that we live in is falling apart', a reference to our planet succumbing to, perhaps, nuclear annihilation, general neglect or, presciently, climate disaster. The title refrain works as a kind of pre-chorus, summing up how, since the beginning of time, humans have been 'on a mission to ...' or in 'a glorious contest to find the invincible one'.

The first chorus then, with its rousing melody – 'And I will know everything there is' – seems to be sung by God himself or, at least, one of his representatives. For the first time, Finn chooses to speak using God's voice, rather than speculate as a believer: 'Goodbye to you and your money. And I will go anywhere you say if you take away all the cameras'. God claims that, after all your searching, he will be there to help but with a few caveats. In the second chorus, Finn is making an editorial comment about preferring to pray in private and for free. Typical of him to see both perspectives, but in this case, he appears to be taking sides.

This song also contains the shortest bridge, lyrically, in the Crowded House discography: 'Okay, we're lucky, but then again'. Straight to the point while still casting a big shadow on the question of belief.

'Time Immemorial' has a similar feel and attitude to 'How Will You Go', which could explain why it didn't make it onto *Woodface*. Both songs were deemed worthy of closing an album, but 'How Will You Go', with its dreamy, cautionary message, seemed more appropriate for the double-threat of *Woodface*'s Finn brothers. 'Time Immemorial' is more of a folk song that tends to mesh better with *Afterglow*'s collection of misfits.

Time On Earth (2007)

Personnel
Neil Finn: guitar, Wurlitzer, vibraphone, piano, lead and backing vocals
Nick Seymour: bass, autoharp, backing vocals
Mark Hart: piano, keyboards, guitar, backing vocals
Matt Sherrod: drums, backing vocals
Additional musicians:
Ethan Johns: drums, sitar, guitar, hurdy-gurdy, string arrangements, backing vocals
Johnny Marr: guitars, backing vocals
Rikki Gooch: drums
Eddie Rayner: harmonium
Sharon Finn: backing vocals
Elroy Finn: guitars
Liam Finn: backing vocals
Beth Rowley: vocals on 'Transit Lounge'
Joey Waronker: drums
Jay Joyce: guitar
Don McGlashan: euphonium, backing vocals
Gavin Wright: strings
Isobel Griffiths: strings
Richard Watkins: French horn
Joseph Lindsay: horns
Isaac McNeill: horns
Scott Towers: horns
Producer: Ethan Johns, Steve Lillywhite ('People Are Like Suns' produced by Finn/Seymour) Engineer: Ethan Johns, Neil Baldock, Jonathan Shakhovskoy, Ryan Freeland
Assistant Engineers: Dave Paul, Helen Atkinson
Mixer: Ethan Johns, Tchad Black, Steve Lillywhite
Assistant mixer: Neil Baldock, Dominic Monks
Recorded between 2006-2007 at Roundhead Studios (NZ), RAK Studios (UK), Real World Studios (UK)
Released in June 2007 on Parlophone (ATO in the US and Canada)
Running time: 58:31
Highest chart position UK: 3, US: 46, Australia: 1, Canada: 38
All songs by Neil Finn, unless otherwise specified

***Time On Earth*, Crowded House's fifth studio release – not including *Afterglow* – began life as a Neil Finn solo album. After all, it had been over ten years since the band officially ended their career with the giant farewell concert in the forecourt of Sydney's famous opera house. Paul Hester's death in 2005 by suicide was in the recent past, and as a way of working through the loss of his friend, Finn started writing and recording. He invited his old**

bandmate Nick Seymour to play some bass, and before long, they began considering the work as a Crowded House record.

Finn said in the 2023 Zoom conversation:

> I'm proud of that record. It is a sad record but really well-rounded. I don't listen to it often, but when I do, there's definitely an ache coming directly from having lost Paul. And it was the spur; we felt like we had to provide some kind of rituals for ourselves to make sense of that. We couldn't just leave a big black full stop. It did bring Nick and me back together and felt like we were putting some good feelings out. We were paying our respects to our fallen comrade.

Finn discovered his recording sessions with Nick Seymour and producer/drummer Ethan Johns were verging into Crowded House territory. He recalled Mark Hart, who subsequently enlisted drummer Matt Sherrod and, as Crowded House Mach II, they recorded the rest of the tracks with producer Steve Lillywhite.

It marks a time when Crowded House went from being the loveable musical imps frolicking on all the video stations to mature musicians making thoughtful music regardless of any critical acceptance. Their fans demonstrated their enthusiastic appetite for the band – released 14 years after *Together Alone*, it was a long welcome surprise – but the singles rarely got any airtime. Still, this is an album that exhibits quality songwriting and superbly constructed songs.

As the band's primary songwriter, Finn proves with *Time On Earth* that he is constantly evolving his craft. He is always striving for the perfect marriage of melody and lyric and doesn't shy away from difficult subjects for inspiration.

The majority of these songs started, as most Crowded House songs do, as demos recorded by Neil alone. Despite the creative input by Mitchell Froom and other producers, Finn was frequently happy enough with his demos to, at the very least, envision how the finished album would sound. He spoke about this during the 2023 Zoom conversation:

> Every album has a collection of demos attached to it. And some demos I listen to and think we didn't really get them better. We made them different. But there's something essential about the way they were written. They're less finished in some cases, but there's something about the original atmospheres of some of my home demos that I prefer to the way the records turned out. If you listen to the bonus disc for the album *Time On Earth*, you will find many demos which I prefer but only for their atmosphere. The demo of 'Don't Stop Now' is a good example.

Time On Earth is dedicated to the memory of Paul Hester.

'Nobody Wants To'

A despondent song with an uplifting melody, this is vintage Neil Finn. 'Nobody Wants To' is a meditation on the fear of acknowledging other peoples' pain.

As an album opener, it sets an austere tone for *Time On Earth*. First, the solo guitar strums simple chords, followed by drums, bass, a second guitar and selective piano fills, the intro sounding very much like any classic country song. Seymour's bass is contemplative even before Finn starts to sing, his voice typically warm and welcoming even while singing about a grim scenario.

The first verse outlines the worst: things are looking so dire that our narrator can't get much lower. 'Down on the ocean floor, that's where I'm heading for ...' At the 45-second mark, Finn is already at the chorus. In the starkest of terms – half warning, half confession – he lays bare what anyone asking for help might expect: 'Nobody wants to think about it. Nobody wants to talk about it. Nobody protects you'.

All at once, Finn is reminding us that, fundamentally, we are all on our own. It's a scary proposition, yet Finn's typically melodic interpretation suggests something quite the opposite. If we can only rely on ourselves, he suggests, then that should be embraced. In so doing, we have already taken the first step to digging ourselves out of the depths. At the end of the second chorus, after the refrain, 'Nobody protects you', he sings the most positive sounding 'Yeah', holding the note for more than a bar, far longer than expected. Then, 'For all I know,' he sings in the bridge, 'I might not get home. But I found out if we open it up we could work this out'. He's looking for a solution.

Mark Hart's selective use of lap steel contributes to the sonic lament that echoes through the song. It's a texture consistent in Crowded House during Hart's tenure in the band, which, in this case, works to tremendous effect.

Uniquely, in the outro chorus, a new character is introduced. 'Everything he told you is wrong', Finn sings. Who is 'he'? Maybe he's the mysterious 'nobody' we keep hearing about, the disembodied spirit who offers no protection. Or he's an oblique reference to Paul Hester (whose presence will be felt more explicitly later in the album) and his claims that everything was fine. Or possibly it's yet another example of Finn's bumpy relationship with God.

'Don't Stop Now'

Finn talked to Jeremy Ansell for the 2016 Deluxe Edition release about the inspiration for 'Don't Stop Now', written during a time living near Bath, England:

> Sharon decided to drive a car in the country lanes. It descended into an incredibly dark and stormy night, as the song says. She got horribly lost and rang me a bit distressed. I had to guide her in and after I'd got her back to

> the house and she'd calmed down, I played her the song I'd been writing and said all I was lacking was a title, which she then came up with.

So, 'Don't Stop Now' is essentially a true story. But can it be more than just a retelling of lovers connecting? Of one rescuing the other from peril? 'God knows where the satellite's taking us, I can't tell what's right in front of us'.

But soon after, the song transforms from a rescue mission into documenting Finn writing the song in real time. He sings, 'Don't stop now', as a message to Sharon and also to himself. Her misfortune is his treasure trove, the discovery of a new melody and a compelling lyric to match. He repeats the refrain as a steady reminder that you have to stay in the flow, sometimes at the expense of other things, to fully receive the muse's inspiration. If Finn's account above is any proof, Sharon may have also played a willing part in the creation of the song.

There is even the suggestion that Finn might have been suffering from some kind of writer's block, as the outro vocal sings in an uncharacteristic monotone: 'Restless and hopeful in the silence I wait with a blank piece of paper on the top of my head, and all I want is something I can write about'. So, as he carefully wishes his love home, he is simultaneously relishing the song he's crafting out of her absence. His guilt is palpable – 'Is the devil gonna track me down?' – and he suggests that 'sometimes you have to turn the wrong way round'; she must remain lost in order for him to complete this song. Still, he continues to be helpful: 'Travel through a tunnel in the trees, just remember that's how you get to me'.

At 133 bpm, 'Don't Stop Now' is one of the most upbeat Crowded House songs ever released as a single. Its tempo and simple 4/4 rock rhythm drive the song forward with the same resolve Sharon was driving with. The urgency continues to build, especially in the last part of the bridge – 'There's no number on the house' – which is driven by pounding piano chords and pedalling bass. It's a well-arranged union between music and lyric. The verse melody starts mainly horizontally, but, with the help of Johnny Marr's guitar, it quickly expands into another soaring Finn hook with 'But I hang on every word', never letting go of its vertical projection.

'Don't Stop Now', the first single from *Time On Earth*, is a captivating song both in narrative and delivery. In this collection of melancholy songs, it is one of the most uplifting moments on the album.

'She Called Up'

'She Called Up' is the most obvious and direct song relating to his old friend, Paul. One can imagine Finn hanging up the phone and immediately writing down the lyric, 'She called up and gave me the news'. For everything taken away, there lies an opportunity.

It starts with the chorus, which includes the line, 'It made me so sad, sad, sad. There was nothing I could do'. Finn's choice of melody, in keeping with his wont, sounds positively bubbly while he sings these words. He told Jeremy Ansell for the 2016 Deluxe Edition:

> It is couched in an incredibly upbeat set of clothes. I don't think I could have sung it otherwise.

The second section uses the same melody as the chorus but acts more as a verse. Here, Finn offers the most genuinely heartbreaking moment of the song: 'I can never repay you now for what you gave to me'.

The second section shifts dramatically from major to the relative minor (each major key is related to a minor key that shares the same sharpened or flattened notes, just played in a different order; in this case, Eb major and C minor) as Finn sings rather more ethereally about this moment: 'A whisper that can blow a chasm wide … Pushed apart the mountains and the tide. It took us all'. Later on, the third section – a second sort of bridge – throws his grief high – 'But truth is a mortal blow' – acknowledging Hester's inner turmoil and obvious pain before landing on a soft blanket of hope with 'There's something better now'.

The second single from *Time On Earth*, 'She Called Up' failed to achieve any significant charting success. It is both jolly and gloomy, one of Finn's signature tricks. The rising melody line of 'She called up …' is combined with calliope-like keyboard fills in the A sections, followed closely by spooky 'la-la-la's over the minor chords. At the coda, these two contrasting elements interlock in a high-energy but emotionally ambiguous ending.

'Say That Again'

The narrator of 'Say That Again' has understood what it means to be a man. Finn has captured the life-changing moment when a comment, perhaps unintentionally, bursts into an epiphany. Finn acknowledges that definitions of masculinity have wobbled like jelly for centuries. Men continue to have to deal with the notion of a manhood that includes toughness, virility, power and earning potential, as well as chivalry, attentiveness and romance – a cross between Machiavelli and Valentino. In short, masculinity was something no man could ever live up to completely.

Then, he falls in love and one day 'there on the shore, the girl that I adore' tells him something that, over time, he is left to figure out. Exactly what she says is never revealed in the lyric, but ultimately, he discovers in its most simple sense, 'I know, you got to fight the plan. You got to bend the rules. I know, you got to be your own man'. No matter how you define it, he learns that being yourself is the key. This is what will ultimately make him more attractive, he hopes.

Finn shifts between major and minor chords even more than usual here, nearly line by line. It results in the sound of decision-making, waffling, back and forth between black and white, between yes and no, all the while trying to determine what kind of man he wants to be. It is clearly not an easy decision: 'Midnight is standing in the shadows. This haunting is a reckless escape'. Still, he tries to be the man he wants to be even if he is breaking the so-called rules set by centuries of masculinity.

The groove and feel laid down by the band – a gentler version of 'Don't Stop Now' – are perfect for this song – dramatic and decisive with a hint of worry. There is a minimal dynamic shift between the verse and chorus aside from the addition of extra guitar in the chorus. Only at the bridge, which switches to 6/4 time starting at 2:38, is there any change in intensity. It's brought in again at the coda at 4:19 to accommodate Finn's epiphany: 'Let's go on making moments last a lifetime. We live on in the promises we keep'.

It's one of the standout songs on *Time On Earth*. Finn concurred in the 2023 Zoom conversation:

> It's one of my favourites. We did play it on that tour and I always really loved playing it. Something about the atmosphere and the melody is really compelling for me. It was never going to be a single. At that point, I think we were divergent from what commercial radio was playing.

'Pour Le Monde'

In a career of writing McCartney-esque songs, 'Pour Le Monde' proves to be Finn's most Lennon-like composition. In one of his rare piano ballads, Finn moves his fingers over the keys in Lennon's distinctive, deliberate style, at once crude and delicate. In this instance, it adds to this song's straightforward melody and low-key delivery.

'Pour Le Monde' is more of a big-picture observation than what Finn normally relies on. What started, according to his account, as a response to having witnessed an anti-war protest in Paris evolved into a tapestry of images suggesting we are minor players on this planet. He wants us to remember that we can prioritise things 'for the world, not for the war'. References to some big-picture contributors include the Wim Wenders film *Wings Of Desire* – 'He imagines the world as the angel ascending' – Viktor Frankl, the Austrian psychologist who wrote *Man's Search For Meaning* – 'And he tries to believe that his life has a meaning' – and Paul Hester – 'He's so low you'll never know'. These external references contribute to the lyric's focus on Finn's outer world, not simply his own account of it.

The strings that enter the third verse lift the song to a greater emotional level after the understated beginning. They continue for the duration and wind the song up at 4:30 with a soft coda to piano accompaniment. The song ends on a melancholy note despite Finn's efforts, as usual, to spin an uplifting tone to a rather dark lyric.

'Pour Le Monde' is another example of Finn's overuse of characters, noted here by way of pronouns. There is 'I', 'You' and 'He'. Generally, 'You' seems to be used in the rhetorical sense, as in 'When you listen for good' ('When one listens for good'). But the relationship between 'I' and 'He' remains unclear.

It was chosen as the third single released from *Time On Earth*.

'Even A Child' (Neil Finn/Johnny Marr)
Johnny Marr's distinctive jangly Rickenbacker 330 takes pride of place on this track. Co-written by Marr and Finn, 'Even A Child' is inevitably the most guitar-reliant song on *Time On Earth*, perhaps the most since 'Locked Out' on *Together Alone*. On this album of subtle, soft-spoken songs, it appears heavier than it actually is.

Finn shares his memory of the sessions with Marr, taken from the *Time On Earth* EPK (electronic press kit):

> He had his daughter, Sonny, singing on it and she is still, in fact, on the track, although there are other voices in there. There was something about the sound of her sweet voice that reminded me that certain truths are known by children and forgotten by adults quite regularly. When you get given a present or a gift or anything, you don't waste it.

It starts as a straight-ahead guitar rocker – like R.E.M. or The Lemonheads to the tune of Tom Petty – in G major before a descending change to F major and then E minor.

The lyric advocates for keeping the lines of communication open, a common theme. This time, Finn focuses on broken promises – 'A promise is only given once' – and the misleading sincerity of best intentions – 'You know I meant it well, but who was it meant to help'. There is also the notion of music as a universal language that children and adults alike can speak: 'There's nothing like waking up in some foreign town. Music is a call to prayer wailing out of speakers in the marketplace'.

Ultimately, Finn suggests, remembering the simple things over 'the ebb and flow of my life' is the key to happiness. More than once, he uses the word 'believe', like a promissory note given from one to another.

There is a lot to enjoy in this quintessential guitar pop song, including Marr's guitar, the verse harmonies and octave vocals in the chorus. But Seymour's buoyant bass line is the unsung hero, dancing around the chords with the kind of child-like freedom championed in this song.

'Heaven That I'm Making'
Some people may believe that Heaven, as a destination and/or a concept, is a place of our own making. That is, we each create our own heaven on Earth while we can. It's surely a concept Finn has explored during his life, and certainly during his career, with a series of songs ('When You Come', 'There Goes God', 'Sacred Cow', etc) that derive insight from his own religious upbringing.

Similarly, 'Heaven That I'm Making' – like much of *Time On Earth* – is imbued with the memory of Paul Hester. This time, Finn could be channelling Hester's voice as he grapples with ideas about his life and his afterlife: 'This heaven that I'm making, it can't come quickly enough' and 'Right on the brink, I end up losing it'.

The lyric swims in a stream of doubt – whether it's better to stay in the life we know or, instead, rely on an afterlife that we might be able to control ourselves. Perhaps most telling is the final stanza, which ends suspended on beat one: 'If there is hell on earth, there must be heaven too. Both in one place and not a second to lose'.

Like many Crowded House songs, it starts with the acoustic guitar. It's quickly joined by an electric piano and some ethereal fills on horns. For a song with quite a bit of chordal movement, Seymour's bass is kept simple and out of the way. An awkward, loping 6/8 time creates a mood of someone limping around looking for answers to unanswerable questions: 'Plead with my saint'. Originally created during sessions with drummer Joey Waronker (Beck, R.E.M.), the final drum track was played by co-producer Ethan Johns.

The placement of this song on the album begins a trilogy of songs where the mood is distinctly contemplative on the theme of loss and longing.

'A Sigh'

As his creative output continued in the wake of Hester's death, a song like 'A Sigh' might have been inevitable. Finn never shied away from songs about death ('Hole In The River', 'She Goes On', etc.), but here, he appeals to the world, his god or the ether: 'What else can I do?' He summed it up in the 2023 Zoom conversation:

> It had a deep atmosphere. I was trying to give words to the unspoken. I got Don McGlashan to sing some BVs on it. He's got a lovely, melancholy sound in his voice, which really helped it.

With 'A Sigh', Finn creates a sonic interpretation of an actual sigh, both musically and lyrically. It features the most minimal arrangement of any Crowded House song: primarily a keyboard pad reminiscent of a choir of voices, softly exhaling, a quietly strummed acoustic guitar with some Wurlitzer and fluttering electric guitar sounds. Over this, Finn gently croons the lyrics to three short verses.

The only recognisable refrain is the repetition of 'A sigh', sung four times, where Finn once again uses the major sixth interval to great effect. The word 'sigh' hangs in the air, almost indefinitely, soaring above 'the deepest well' from which it sprung. Verse one's sigh is an unspoken connection between the narrator and the person he misses. In verse two, the sigh emanates from his friend as he waits for 'loneliness to end, no changing the story now'. The sigh returns to the narrator in the third verse when, after losing his friend, he admits, 'this show is not fooling anyone, but it's all for you'.

Most poignantly, the final line of the lyric is a sigh of helpless acceptance that he must bear this loss: 'But I think your mind is made up'. As the choir fades out, we hear the ghostly tone of Finn's sigh ringing out on the F# – over D major – acting as a virtual segue into the next song.

'Silent House' (Neil Finn/Emily Robison/Martie Maguire/Natalie Maines)
'These walls ...' Finn sings to open 'Silent House', echoing the lingering notes of 'A sigh ...'. The word 'walls' is sung on the same F# note, but this time using a perfect fourth interval over an F# minor chord.

Co-written with the members of The Chicks (formerly the Dixie Chicks, the country music trio who changed their name in 2020) in a single writing session, the song was first recorded by the trio in 2006. A year later, it was included on *Time On Earth* and sounds in every way like a Crowded House song, particularly with its razor-sharp melody, perfect harmonies and melding of major and minor key centres.

While 'Silent House' is specifically about The Chicks' Natalie Maines' grandmother living with Alzheimer's disease, Finn sings his version with the weariness of someone overcome by the weight of watching a loved one slip away. Consider the way he sings, 'Who do we become without knowing where we started from', stopping to take a breath halfway through the word 'started' as if he is worn out by the grief.

The song is propelled by a distorted electric guitar softly in the mix, acting as a kind of drone. Coupled with Finn's voice recorded close to the microphone, the effect is both rasping and intimate. Drums start to keep time in the pre-chorus – 'Everything that you made by hand' – starting a build-up through suspended chords over C# that resolve satisfyingly on the F# major for the chorus.

The chorus – anthemically positive after the contemplative, minor key verses – rings out with more guitar tracks and a glorious affirmation of inter-generational love. Whereas 'A Sigh' was a case of throwing hands up in the air in helplessness, 'Silent House' is about turning despair into an act of love. A child vows to keep the memory of their beloved parent alive while their own memory fails: 'I will try to connect all the pieces you left. I will carry it on and let you forget'. Capturing the bittersweet mood in both lyric and music, 'Silent House' hits the target on every emotional level.

'English Trees'
This is the third song of another quasi-trilogy that includes 'Tall Trees' and 'Help Is Coming' about leaving home and finding a new world. 'English Trees', compared to the other songs in the trilogy, is more sentimental. Written while Finn was living in England and writing songs that would eventually land in *Time On Earth*, he was reflecting on the passage of time exemplified by a

tree's annual transformation. Surely reminders of his mother's journey played a role in his reflections: 'They planted seeds in a faraway land', 'England cries and she plays for him' and 'In Regent's Park I will mourn for you'. Just as he acknowledges the memory of his mother, he also hopes he will be remembered by those he loves: 'Nothing's sadder I know, than the passing of time ... And I must be wise somehow. You won't forget me'. He told Jeremy Ansell for the 2016 Deluxe Edition:

> In England, the seasons are very clearly marked and they also, to some degree, are a constant reflection of the moods of men and women. There must be something that you can understand, or something that you can grasp hold of that gives you a clue as to life in tragic circumstances, but you can't see it at the time.

'English Trees' has no chorus, only a refrain of 'English trees in my garden' acting as a kind of signpost that a new section is starting. Set to a 'Weather With You' tempo, there is very little dynamic variation in the arrangement: acoustic guitar, bass, drums and an organ pad (sounding like a bagpipe drone throughout). The simple instrumentation and performance give it a 1960s feel, similar to The Byrds or Buffalo Springfield's folk-rock.

'Walked Her Way Down'

A great vocal performance highlights this simple march of a song (the drums enter halfway through the first verse) full of hooky melodic moments. Short lyrical lines in the verses, delivered by Finn like thought bubbles, position the narrator as disembodied. Indeed, as he describes what he sees in front of him, he's also observing himself.

For the first time since 'Mean To Me' – album one, track one – Finn writes explicitly about being a musician. In 'Walked Her Way Down', it's his view from the stage that provides insight into this perspective. As he watches one person walk toward the stage, perhaps to connect directly with him or simply to be closer to the music source, he reflects on positions of power, privilege, creativity and what he has learned in his career.

It uses a tight minor key progression in the verse that, tied to sustained guitar chords and raspy baritone saxophone deep in the mix, creates a claustrophobic atmosphere. The staccato verse opens up into a welcoming, lusher chorus, highlighted by a shift to a major key centre on the line that brings this song to life: 'And when you're in the moment everything you want is right'.

Each chorus ends with a reference to 'the drummer': first, 'counting out the start', then he 'makes the same mistake' and, finally, 'always comes in late'. It's unclear whether Finn is referring to one drummer specifically (Hester, maybe) or drummers in general, who are often the butt of jokes from and about musicians.

Another lyrical evolution is the second line of the chorus, 'And I'm happy to be here tonight', something many frontmen will say to their audiences. But by the third chorus, he sings on the first line, 'And we happen to be here tonight,' which plays on the near rhyme but also suggests that this moment he's witnessing could be any random concert at any time.

The bridge is used effectively here as the drums cut out and Finn sings over a lone piano, 'And my eyes are on the shape that is captured in the light'. It seems to be the one moment when he is inside his own head again, no longer just watching himself. It's a section that works so well against the relentless march that it's brought back again at the end, followed by the ultimate line, 'And I want to feel her weightless grasp upon my heavy life'. He acknowledges that there is a relationship between him and his audience, both as a group and individually.

'Transit Lounge'

A busy song about chaotic travel and the disconnected feelings experienced in airport lounges, Finn reflects on conversations with strangers as busses of people arrive, filling the space with more people to breathe on.

The song opens with an unusual electronic sound – kind of like a deep groan from a theremin – and a recorded voice announcing travel updates in German, which return later in the song.

There is the mysterious character of 'Her', with whom the narrator shares secrets: 'Talk to her, that's right. It could mean more than you think ... She's the only one who knows where you're from and where you've been'. The voice of 'Her' is supplied by British singer Beth Rowley, who was recording in the adjacent studio during the *Time On Earth* sessions. Her vocals weave in and out of Finn's narrative like a spirit, sometimes an octave away, other times in harmony and providing ghostly 'oohs-and-aahs' in the uplifting middle section. She is the persistent memory of the transitory encounter.

The middle section starting at 1:58 – a kind of extended bridge that simulates a soaring plane – is the highlight of the song. While the bulk of the verses and chorus bounce along in C minor and F minor like a 1980s pop song, it then takes off into a smooth, soaring section with a tailwind in Eb major: 'I spent a lot of time in the transit lounge, and I wasn't sure where I was going now'. The section ends with the sense of freedom while travelling, with only your own wits to rely on: 'You better make sure you don't sleep too sound, there'll be no announcements made'.

In the end, 'Her' has perhaps moved on, but instead, we are introduced to 'the tallest man alive' who goes for a Thai foot massage before his flight. The cycle of people continues despite the song's abrupt ending.

Melodically, 'Transit Lounge' shares characteristics with songs on *Dreamers Are Waiting* (compare it to 'Bad Times Good' or 'Too Good For This World'), still 14 years away. This is an early signal that Finn's songwriting style and melodic sensibilities were evolving.

'You Are The One To Make Me Cry'

In 2007, New Zealand Navy diver Rob Hewitt drifted away from his fellow divers during a shift gathering crayfish. For the next 75 hours, he treaded water, surviving on the animals he'd caught, without fresh water to drink and deep in the grip of hallucinations. He thought he was home; he thought he was already dead.

When this story hit the news, Neil Finn set it to music he'd already been working on. Putting himself in Hewitt's shoes, he imagined what it would be like to witness your own life leaving you, your body already starting to decompose from the saltwater while your mind plays cruel tricks on you.

Mainly arranged with Finn on electric piano and some gentle strings, the song lilts over the waves in a slow waltz. The verses share the hallucinatory feeling Hewitt might have felt while adrift almost half a mile off the New Zealand coast – 'Told everyone I know that I was sorry, and I heard them all singing ... Make circles in time, a spiderweb spinning' – until, ultimately, amid moments of lucidity, he was prepared to die: 'I'll let this wave take me and draw me down'.

Finn stakes a claim that Hewitt's main source of strength must have been thoughts of his loved ones. As the chorus says: 'You're the one to make me cry ... my thoughts keep returning to you'. Then the gut-wrenching admission: 'But consciousness is fading fast'.

Although Hewitt was finally rescued after more than three days adrift, Finn leaves us at the dreadful moment when rescue planes flew overhead but couldn't see him. He trails off in a barely audible falsetto: 'If you could hear me cry for help. But I lift my head up to the sky. But the planes that were circling now have gone'.

The song is in A minor and refrains from using flattened sevenths or bluesy notes, giving the song its directness.

'People Are Like Suns'

The perfect finale to *Time On Earth*, 'People Are Like Suns' encompasses many of the themes on this melancholy album: death and longing, helplessness, a troubled mind and the slow, circular passage of time. Stimulated by a moment in the Ian McEwan novel *Saturday* (about a neurosurgeon whose tumultuous day off provides him with cause for reflection), Finn's mind was clearly already in the mode of writing songs laden with these existential motifs.

Early on, Finn sings with the same weariness heard in 'A Sigh', 'Silent House' and 'You Are The One To Make Me Cry'. As the song builds in intensity, so does his vocal performance, but only enough to show a bolstered acceptance of his observations. It stops just short of being either overly dramatic or sentimental.

The plaintive verses stutter as the protagonist tries to gather his thoughts. The centrepiece of the song is a lyric that reflects on how fleeting our time is on this earth, a theme for the entire album: 'And they come and they go in. the blink of an eye'. Coming out of the Eb major verse, it shifts to B major as the vertical melody sounds more resigned to the reality of life's fragility. Then, it steps from the B major down to E major on the payoff line, 'People are like suns, they keep burning up inside … breathing into life all that's good in us'. We are, after all, both created and nurtured by those before us and are also the keepers of their memories.

Intriguer (2010)

Personnel
Neil Finn: guitar, piano, lead and backing vocals
Nick Seymour: bass
Mark Hart: piano, keyboards, guitar
Matt Sherrod: drums
Additional musicians:
Don McGlashan: mandolin, tambourine, guitar, euphonium
Sharon Finn: vocals
Liam Finn: guitar
Lisa Germano: violin
Jon Brion: guitar, backing vocals
Jim Scott: piano, percussion
Michael McClintock: violin
Greg Leisz: pedal steel
Producer: Jim Scott, Neil Finn
Engineer: Jim Scott, Jordan Stone
Assistant Engineer: Charles Pagler
Additional Recording: Brian Crosby
Mixer: Jim Scott, Kevin Dean
Recorded between May and August 2009, Roundhead Studios (Auckland), Exchequer Studios (Dublin), PLYRZ Studios (LA)
Released in June 2010 on Fantasy, UMGI
Running time: 40:19
Highest chart position: UK: 12, US: 50, Australia: 1
All songs by Neil Finn, unless otherwise specified

This is an album of two halves. The first five songs show the worldly side of Neil Finn – a man who has travelled and spent the bulk of his adult life on a stage. It shows his unique observations of people from various perspectives with a big-picture sensibility to the songs. Flip the record over and side two showcases the intimate side of the songwriter – personal songs about people he loves and the seemingly endless insecurities that surround his relationships with them.

With arrangements that layer instruments in sophisticated ways, it is a more densely produced album than any other by Crowded House. Producer Jim Scott's experience working with such acts as Tom Petty, Foo Fighters and The Rolling Stones introduced a more pugnacious edge than previously used. Even the softer songs maintain a certain coarseness that was not heard on earlier releases.

The result is a sonic blending of Finn's inimitable melodies, the band's unique arrangements and a promise that Crowded House's creative juices were well and truly flowing.

Of *Intriguer*, Finn told Will Harris of *Bullz-Eye* in 2010:

> The intuition and instinct were back and we'd spent a good amount of time working the songs out from scratch together, road-testing them. I think it has a great presence to it in my mind, but this feels more like a band record. It feels like everyone's got a bigger part and the character of the band is more on show.

In the 2023 Zoom conversation, he said:

> It didn't get a lot of attention at the time. It's only years later you learn if the songs endure or the albums endure. But I was really proud of it when we made it. We had done a lot of touring before that and played a lot of those songs on stage. They changed quite a lot when we recorded them with Jim Scott. Some of the fans who had got used to the old live versions were almost upset that we'd gone ahead and changed them. So that was an unusual experience. We don't normally have the songs ready before touring. Compared to *Time On Earth*, it's a more upbeat record.

Drummer Matt Sharrod finally got to inject his own style into the Crowded House sound. A more relaxed, looser player than both Hester and Peter Jones, Sharrod incorporated impromptu fills and spent more time on the cymbals than his predecessors. On *Time On Earth*, he had very little to do, only appearing on four songs. But he accepted the gig on the condition he was made a permanent member, so on the ensuing tour, he was able to develop a style that would suit Crowded House. Sharrod spoke on the *Intriguer* EPK of sitting in Paul Hester's drum seat, now two albums and one tour later:

> I don't feel like I've stepped into his shoes because I didn't really know that much about the band when I joined. So it wasn't as daunting, but as I met the fans and played the music, I definitely realised my responsibility in the band.

Furthermore, Mark Hart proves again how skilled he is at providing colour to the main arrangement with keyboard and guitar textures.

Intriguer sounds very much like a new Crowded House – which it is. There is a novel spirit on this album that embraces getting older – Finn was now in his 50s – and having moved on from many of the issues that would have engulfed their youth. New melodic and harmonic tendencies that started showing up during *Time On Earth* in songs like 'Transit Lounge' and 'You Are The One To Make Me Cry' continue to feature here. 'Isolation' and 'Inside Out', for example, would have felt at home on the upcoming *Dreamers Are Waiting* album.

Yet, despite the step forward, Finn was less committed to the future of Crowded House as an ongoing entity, which resulted in him shutting down his band for the second time after the tour to support *Intriguer*. He told John Aizlewood of *Mojo* in the June 2024 issue:

To be honest, I'd reached a dead end in my mind. We'd tried to record after *Intriguer*, but I couldn't finish anything with that lineup. It felt like a good time to stop.

'Saturday Sun'

A strong album opener. Despite 'Saturday Sun' being yet another song about madness, it sets the tone musically for a more upbeat recording than *Time On Earth*. It was released as the first single from *Intriguer*, perhaps hoping that sharing a tempo and feel with 'Don't Stop Now' would bring similar success, but it failed to chart in any market.

The first sounds are bottom-heavy drums and distorted bass that show Crowded House's rarely accentuated but often present rock credentials. The vocals enter along with Mark Hart's jangly keyboard, sung with Finn's inimitable warmth but doubled with a synthesised voice (via Vocoder), giving it a raspier sound to balance the bass and drums.

The protagonist looms like some 'Aqualung' (Jethro Tull) figure, possibly homeless, not in his right mind, with the potential for even more perverse tendencies. Like some earlier songs, Finn inexplicably uses various pronouns – 'He', 'You' and 'I' – in the narrative. The difference is that in 'Saturday Sun', they all might be referring to the same person. He says explicitly at the top of the first chorus, 'He's insane', followed by, 'Inside his mind lies all of space and time'. In the second verse: 'My head is alright, was the darkest of nights'. In the bridge, which describes what he might be looking for out there ('...the revolution maybe, or visions of the underworld'), he says, 'But when you saw the first light then you know it's alright'.

Yet, despite the sinister undertones, this is a happy person. There is emphasis on the sun that appears on this Saturday, which is 'calling on the day 'til the clouds get blown away'. If things have been looking bleak, 'It's all about to change'.

After the bridge, when Finn uses his screaming voice to great effect, there is a six-bar break of 'Na na na na na's followed by a terrific six-bar guitar solo at 2:15. Those 12 bars let the song breathe and bring a welcome dynamic shift. With the discovery of the revelation (in the bridge), the final verse shows the relief that 'the nightmare is done. And in time he waits, colours up the sky. Make the darkness come to life'.

'Archer's Arrows'

Sharrod's drumming opens the song with a military-style drumroll that settles into a four-on-the-floor march, suggesting a platoon of archers is about to let loose their ammunition. Electric piano joins in followed by some creative bass work from Seymour.

Three distinct sections – verse, pre-chorus and chorus – provide a clear arc to the musical narrative of this song. There are three or four keyboard parts and no distinguishable guitar can be heard, making this one of the more unique Crowded House arrangements to date. Finn explained in the *Intriguer* EPK: 'It's a metaphor. Lofty ambitions and your aim suddenly fall short.'

After 'the archer fires away' in the pre-chorus – which includes Sharon Finn's distinctive voice – Finn lays out the flaws in aiming high: 'The whole façade is wearing thin, we'll just paper over cracks'. He recognises that, despite the cautionary note, people will still continue to strive for bigger and better things: 'We live to fight another day. See the arrows fly'.

The singable chorus features densely harmonised vocals sharing a descending melody line, sung over thrilling piano cascades that together elicit the images of arrows soaring in an arc toward their target.

'Amsterdam'

This is an almost comical recounting of an ill-fated trip to the Dutch city. Whatever could go wrong did go wrong: the queue for the Van Gogh exhibit was too long, there were no tables at the restaurant, it rained, the streets were filled with 'a million people on a protest march' and men dressed in grey trying to bilk tourists of their money. He begins to think there is a conspiracy against him. Set to a slow, dirge-like groove, 'Amsterdam's melody feels so good while everything within the song goes bad.

One of the strongest choruses on *Intriguer*, the escapade finally sees the narrator admit that 'They're the darkest days of a free man'. Though he tries to see the bright side of this unfortunate scenario amid 'every temptation and device, all the diamonds and the spice', he has to confess, 'I would give anything for the sight of an honest man'. He's not doing much to boost the standing of Dutch tourism.

The final pre-chorus harkens back to 'There Goes God' with its representation of God walking the earth: 'And the Lord walked in with a monocle and lips so thin. Saw the barman wink as he poured his brandy'. This suggests that everyone knows the truth about what's going on except for the narrator; that maybe there really is a conspiracy and it starts all the way at the top.

The final lyric – 'Who would take profit from the vice of another man' – speaks to Amsterdam's reputation as a place to legally obtain drugs, sex and other illicit cravings.

'Either Side Of The World'

'Amsterdam's sister song, this starts off in a place of joy 'Where the famous have come to be alone'. This 'last resort' location far away from home where you 'pay the maximum rate' sounds too good to be true: 'When you're in luck the world moves with you'.

Yet, this narrator soon confesses, 'Wish I could've held my tongue'. How many times has a celebrity gotten themselves cancelled by speaking without thinking? 'Whatever you want, you turn yourself into. And then,' he sings as the penny drops, 'you're in Hell'.

A lush bridge, with ascending piano and descending guitar, lays it all on the line: 'Luxury and leisure never meant pleasure'.

At 2:40 there begins another Crowded House false ending – a brief hiatus from reality into a (medicated) side trip. Ethereal keyboard pads warping around E minor swirl around with solo accordion notes until the piano and percussion re-enter at 3:12, followed by angelic voices. We're brought back to the here and now with 'Wish I could have held my tongue', a final chorus, and then, in true Crowded House fashion, the song finishes on a second bridge.

It's perhaps Finn's finest vocal performance on *Intriguer*. The arrangement is busy but low in intensity, which allows for the melody line to work as the true highlight of the song.

The intro shares a feel and tonality with Harry Nilsson's 'Everybody's Talkin''. Whereas Nilsson's song starts with arpeggiated guitars and proceeds in a bouncy country swing, 'Either Side Of The World' begins with tribal-sounding drums before guitar and piano join in. Yet, the similarity in quality of the two songs is undeniable.

'Falling Dove'

Inspired by stories in Russian spy novels Neil Finn read as a child and was reminded of during a train ride from Moscow to St Petersburg, 'Falling Dove' has images of shadowy souls, mysterious intrigue and love fraught with possible danger. Lines like 'One loose word, a revolution' and 'Lift him up, barely breathing' maintain the air of mystery Finn seems to prefer here.

This falling dove might indeed refer to Russia losing its grasp as a peaceful country due to the rising post-Soviet political temperature around this time. The dove, a universal symbol of peace, is portrayed here as fragile and in need of help to prove we are all the same beyond political boundaries. However, considering Finn rarely crosses into political territory in his lyrics, it's more likely that the inspiration is akin to a *Doctor Zhivago*-style love story set during the later Russian Revolution. The dove is asked, 'Do you believe in us like I believe in us ... You keep defending me when I'm behaving badly'.

The narrative continues in a more uplifting, hopeful tone for these lovers as the arrangement evolves from acoustic to electric guitars and pounding piano: 'May the best of fortune bless you. Could any creature be unmoved.'

The final verse, returning to the acoustic setting, is more distinctly set in the present day like a flash forward, drawing a parallel narrative with the historic love affair of the earlier verses. The singer prepares to 'make a rendezvous in Moscow station', but 'the café is closed'. His train then pulls into St. Petersburg, he is feeling lost and forlorn like 'a dead man', then miraculously sees the woman he was meant to meet.

'Falling Dove' is played in a steady mid-tempo 4/4, except in the verses, where the second bar of every four-bar phrase is in 3/4. Although this time change feels completely natural, it actually helps to drive the narrative forward with its short, clipped lines. It uses the uncommon form A, A, B, C, A, with an instrumental tag at the end suggesting it might go to the B or C section again but never does.

'Isolation' (Neil Finn/Nick Seymour/Mark Hart/Matt Sherrod)
As Finn matured, so did his ability to distinguish between the often opposing perspectives in his narratives as they grew ever more refined. In 'Isolation', he admits to a desperate desire to flee loneliness while simultaneously admitting he's found a way to overcome it: 'There's always a way to end this isolation', he sings.

This song doesn't go where it might be expected to go. A slow 6/8 that revolves around a heavily echoed, arpeggiated guitar figure, it starts with Finn and a female voice – Sharon Finn again – vocalising 'oooh'. Neil takes the first verse, identifying the arrival of someone he might want to get closer to: 'Open up your heart, someday you will'. Sharon takes the second verse as she recognises that sometimes people come into our lives unexpectedly out of nowhere, but that she, too, struggles with making connections: 'Though I try, try to find a sign of another life, I am alone'. They sing together, 'One step away from everyone', as they try to end their isolation.

Neil wrote in the Crowded House Club newsletter in 2010:

> Sharon has an innocent approach. Her voice isn't mannered or stylised; it's just a lovely tone – beautiful, simple, honest singing, which I really like, and it suited the song 'Isolation'. She can sound breathy and ethereal, so it worked out really well.

Seymour elaborated on the *Intriguer* EPK:

> She's sung on most of our previous records as a backing vocalist or with little character qualities. This is the first time she's actually sung a duet with Neil.

After a 12-bar guitar solo, they continue together, Neil in falsetto and Sharon an octave down: 'I wish you would take me along to end this isolation'. At this point, the song takes an unexpected left turn, switching to a rock steady 4/4 time, thick with at least three tracks of distorted guitar. In some ways, it's a welcome relief from the steady 6/8 that never changes its dynamic. Neil continues in his falsetto and rock voice until he gets to the final line and sings victoriously: 'And I believe it, that one day you'll step inside'. It's an invitation for her to join him, not to alleviate his isolation but rather so that they'll be isolated together.

'Twice If You're Lucky'
A plaintive piano intro – that never gets repeated – opens this celebratory song about accepting true joy into your life. Whether it's falling in love,

achieving the success of your dreams or, as seems to be the case in this song, having children, other moments of happiness may pale in comparison. Finn wants to share these moments but recognises that perhaps what is meaningful to him may not be the same for others: 'It's a course in philosophy'. Although he believes this, he might not always be able to clearly articulate it, as he sings in the pre-chorus: 'But you know what it means to me, babe. In the course of a history, hey, it all makes sense to me somehow'.

When he gets to the chorus, he states plainly: 'These are times that come only once in your life, or twice if you're lucky'. He is breathing the rarefied air of absolute elation; one of those singular moments that sustains in our memories: 'What if the chance it comes around another time. You risk it all, you take the fall for what you like'.

There are only four chords in this song: E, A, G# minor and B. That's conservative chord usage for Finn. But the result here is a rousing, anthemic, densely produced song with a positive lyric and hooky melody. After the opening piano passage, the song drives forward under its own momentum and doesn't stop until the final chord rings out, along with the echo of Finn singing, 'lucky'.

The melody is simple and catchy, the chorus is memorable, the message is uplifting and the musical tone would fit in with both rock and easy listening stations. At the time of *Intriguer*'s release, however, Crowded House had all but ceased to be a band that radio program directors were seeking new music from.

'Inside Out'

Guitar-heavy, with a simple, marching beat that is sustained from start to finish, 'Inside Out' is an appropriate follow-up to 'Twice If You're Lucky'. The joy realised in the previous song is explored further here, focusing on the pleasure of intimacy: 'You know me back to front. You know exactly what I'm gonna do next'. With maximum energy, the narrator declares his passion as he provides evidence of the connection he's made: 'And I ache for all of your suffering'.

However, in true Finn fashion, that's not the end of it. Although this relationship may be for better or for worse, the narrator finds himself admitting he might ignore their differences: 'The extrovert is always in your face, unaware he's invading your personal space'. This circular logic is laid out explicitly with, 'Circle round the hazy sun. The hazy sun is circling the house'. Ironically, even with this lyrical motif, the song itself is linear through its A, A, B, C, D form, with only the intro and outro matching.

Lacking in dynamic variety and melodically plain for a Finn composition, it's little wonder 'Inside Out' is the least streamed song on *Intriguer* (according to Spotify in 2024). The raspy rhythm guitar's relentless presence becomes tiresome by the song's midpoint and is crying out for some respite.

'Even If'

There are fewer greater pleasures than watching your children grow up. However, Finn acknowledges that this can never happen without you growing older yourself. This lyric beautifully explores that counterbalance, with a strong emphasis on the 'old men' side.

Finn provides some strong lines worthy of any decent parenting manual: 'Things I got so worried about are working out just fine'; 'And nothing good is true unless you find out for yourself'; 'There's a love that can't be found until you set it free'.

In the chorus, he issues a warning to men like him who are getting older and perhaps less able to cling to the kind of parental control they'd become used to. These men are evolving from holding a place of authority to being a mere symbolic patriarch: 'Old men be warned. He can't be helped ... It's not your fault'.

Finn tempers all this angst with his gentle voice and uplifting melody. When he sings, 'It can't be helped' – with four harmony parts soaring on the word 'can't' and stepping up on the word 'helped' – inevitable positive vibrations ensue.

The arrangement harkens back to the days of Crowded House as a trio, using piano, bass and drums as the main instruments, along with string pads and vocals to balance out Finn's angular melody.

'Elephants'

This is one of Finn's purest love songs ever to be featured on a Crowded House record. Wrapping up the family-focused, emotionally bare side two, it's also the finale of *Intriguer*. A more traditional piano ballad than 'Even If', 'Elephants' is another one of Finn's waltzes – like on *Woodface* and *Afterglow* – to be used as an album closer, this one feeling more wistful than previous Finn waltzes.

This narrative starts in a bar at 'the closing hour' where our narrator and his lover are enjoying their last drink. They find themselves huddled together in their own shared isolation, as it were, where the rest of the world – represented by 'a drunk that's sleeping in the corner' – simply shuts them out.

The second verse uses a unique analogy for a love song: 'When elephants come down to the water hole at dusk, they feel the same as us about life'. As the lovers sip their drinks, blissfully ignorant to the rest of the world, they can't escape the fear that 'the alligator waits for his time'. True love, the tipsy narrator declares, even in isolation, can be vulnerable to unexpected peril.

A lovely instrumental section allows the song to breathe while the lovers finish their drinks. Piano and lap steel work together like two voices before moving into the bridge. Simply stated, 'you don't have to say a word, I know what you're thinking' reiterates the sentiment raised in 'Inside Out', but this time, it's only for themselves to hear.

A third verse expresses the singer's vulnerabilities to his love: 'So lost and discontent, I'm looking for a friend I can trust'. At the end of the final chorus, the two lovers toast to their lives together: 'Sweet dreams, make waves, find bliss'. Like a lullaby, a lovely message to end on.

Dreamers Are Waiting (2021)

Personnel
Neil Finn: guitar, piano, keyboards, lead and backing vocals
Nick Seymour: bass, keyboards, backing vocals
Liam Finn: guitar, keyboards, lead and backing vocals
Elroy Finn: drums, guitar, keyboards, backing vocals
Mitchell Froom: keyboards
Additional musicians:
Sharon Finn: backing vocals
Eliza-Jane Barnes: backing vocals
Producer: Crowded House
Engineer: David Boucher, Crowded House
Additional Engineer: Travis Pavur, Wesley Seidman
Mixer: David Boucher
Recorded in 2020 at Valentine Recording Studios (LA), United Recording Studios (LA), home studios (Ireland, NZ, LA)
Released in June 2021 on EMI Australia
Running time: 41:53
Highest chart position UK: 6, US: n/a, Australia: 2, Canada: n/a
All songs by Neil Finn, unless otherwise specified

Crowded House have been a family project from the beginning. From early Finn Brothers compositions that led to the formation of Crowded House to Tim joining the band on *Woodface* to the welcome participation of Sharon, Liam and Elroy Finn throughout. If there had ever been doubt in Neil Finn's mind about maintaining the Crowded House brand, it surely would have been quelled by the notion of it being the family business. As he told *60 Minutes Australia* in 2021 when asked about Liam and Elroy now being fully recognised band members:

> There are all manner of different feelings attached to it. But bands need to have some soul and some spirit, and I don't think there are five people on the planet who feel, live and breathe the Crowded House ethos more than these five. It feels natural, actually.
>
> It's an instinct or an intuition that this was a really good time. Inadvertently, we chose the perfect time to become a band as the world was plunged into such a strange time because we had each other to share the music with, to make a record with – collaboration, companionship, camaraderie, all of the above.

Liam Finn added:

> There's a lot of pride in me and Elroy being able to be part of this with Dad. I sort of dreamed that I'd get to do that one day with them.

This is Crowded House mark III. There's a newer sound on this album that is both familiar and unique. The junior Finns' input is felt throughout, particularly Liam's guitar playing, which comes across as part Roger McGuinn's Rickenbacker and part Ry Cooder's 'Coodercaster'. Mitchell Froom's input as a full-time band member – after years of being a hands-on producer – is major, if not strictly musically, then simply for the love of having him in their midst.

Recording began in Los Angeles after Finn returned from extensive touring as a part of Fleetwood Mac, a two-year partnership that saw Finn filling in for the departed Lindsey Buckingham (with additional help on guitar from The Heartbreakers' Mike Campbell). For many people, it might have seemed an unlikely option, but at the invitation of drummer Mick Fleetwood, Finn jumped at the chance to be a part of another world-class band and explore musical possibilities. As the world shut down in the spring of 2020, the five members of the new Crowded House completed their parts from their disparate home studios on three continents. That they still managed to sound like a band with 'some soul and some spirit' is a testament to their musical skills and their indisputable bond.

In live performances, the presence of the youthful Finns seems to have brought a return to the novel exuberance that ran rampant through the band's early years. Liam has stepped into the role of stage ham and banter partner for his father, just as Paul Hester had done 30 years earlier. Finn reflected on this during the 2023 Zoom conversation:

> They certainly bring a lot to the party. During the most recent tour we did of the US and Canada, it was really evident that the band had grown quite a lot. We are now pushing it out in a really vibrant manner. There's a lot of trust on stage and an ability to step off script and jam. That reminds me of the early days when we were a kind of free entity. We could go off in any direction on stage and we were excited by mistakes and accidents. It's starting to feel like that again.

He then added somewhat poignantly:

> I've been in three bands – Split Enz, Crowded House and Pajama Club – which I regard as real bands in that the sum of the parts created a distinctive sound. The second incarnation of Crowded House became a great band but were not somehow able to move forward in the studio. That takes some aesthetic intermingling that is fresh and suggestive of new frontiers. The current lineup of Crowded House has that feeling.

Finn's voice sounds older and raspier but just as warm as always. His songs continue to explore the larger themes that give him pause, from big-picture issues like freedom and the current global conditions to more intimate ones like interpersonal relationships. The new sound includes the greater use of major chords. Call it a sign of Finn's happiness, but these songs are brighter.

With all this in mind, *Dreamers Are Waiting* is music from a band in their twilight years. Many of the songs lack that musical punch of unforgettable hooks and energy that drenched their earlier recordings. They've lost the 'singability' so prevalent in their first four albums. The melodies are less adventurous throughout and, therefore, less memorable. Awkwardly, nearly every song on *Dreamers Are Waiting* ends unexpectedly, abruptly, as if the band had run out of creative ideas.

As a reunion album of sorts, it's an enjoyable listen, but make sure it's not the only Crowed House album you familiarise yourself with.

'Bad Times Good' (Neil Finn/Liam Finn/Nick Seymour/Elroy Finn)

It reads like an equation – bad X good = a new song. In reality, it's the perfect opener for Crowded House in 2021, the version that blossomed out of the COVID-19 lockdown, because, as Finn sings, 'it looks like some kind of medicine for me'. Take your bad times and make them better.

As Finn continued to demonstrate through *Time On Earth* and *Intriguer*, song form had become less and less prescriptive, Finn preferring instead to focus entirely on melody. With greater frequency, he eschewed the traditional verse-chorus-repeat expectation. This model was pushed further by the fact that Finn commonly changed lyrics in choruses for variety. In 'Bad Times Good', there doesn't appear to be a section that is distinctly a verse or a chorus, yet all the sections work together to build the song. Simply put, it's an A, B, A, B, C, A form. The A section is in 5/4 time, while the rest of the song is in 3/4. It's Finn's first use of the odd time signature on a major Crowded House release.

Though it had been more than a decade since *Intriguer*, we know we're in familiar territory when we get to the bridge. The narrator sings, 'Whether sunlight or shadow falls on me', switching from A minor to A major. His melody continues to rise up the scale on 'You won't come out' as the band change to D minor, then step up to the E major7 on 'Rolling drums they say'. It's melodic, it's the key hook of the song and it's prime Crowded House.

While the band have evolved from a trio in the 1980s to a quartet and then to a quintet (with apologies to guest artists and auxiliary live musicians), the sound has not vastly altered. These five musicians understand that sometimes less is more and the arrangement of 'Bad Times Good' is a great example of that restraint. Based on guitar arpeggios, the rest of the musicians merely serve the song with piano fills, guitar colour and generous amounts of backing vocals.

'Playing With Fire' (Neil Finn/Liam Finn/Elroy Finn/Nick Seymour/ Mitchell Froom)

A percussive guitar count in – very 'Hole In The River' – opens this political commentary wrapped up in social commentary. The narrator of this timely song imagines what it must be like for a globalist corporate cog to cope with the real issues that millennials face: climate change, pandemics and mental health. He appreciates his golden opportunities – 'The chairman's looking out for me and fortune used to favour me' – but still feels that 'the end isn't far away'. He recognises the pushback from his children but denies there is a problem: 'Now some might say we're losing ground. I've never seen such a thing'. He can't shake the feeling he's living on a knife edge, 'playing with fire'. As the outside situation worsens, so does his own: 'My wife is wild in quarantine. The chairman's got it in for me'.

At 1:16, there enters a chorus of brass in unison with some Burt Bacharach-esque 'bah-bah-bah' vocals. This leads to a more realistic admission of humanity's obligations: 'Let's all be quiet, the next generation's talking … be equal to the fight. Be someone saving lives'.

Eventually, the protagonist transforms from hopeless to hopeful, as 'I've never seen such a thing' becomes 'If you believe such a thing, I'll believe such a thing'. Still, the hopefulness stops abruptly as Liam Finn's guitar spins out into an ominous, dissonant whirlpool of doubt and dark string pads segue, appropriately, into the introduction to…

'To The Island'

…the unmistakable second part of the 'Playing With Fire' chapter. 'To The Island' is where this cornered but hopeful character goes when given the opportunity: 'You found me lost in the chaos and confusion. You said it's possible that we can be free'. The island represents freedom from whatever troubles us. It's a place where you answer to no one besides your own conscience and where no evils can reach you. Ultimately, it is the ultimate escape from the cold, soulless cities: 'Come to the island where we can save our souls.'

To a marching tempo, voices chant 'Hey-ey, oh-oh', echoing the voices of the previous song. Finn sings, close to the microphone and double-tracked, of 'the promise of love' (the same promise made in 'Private Universe') and other tastes of hope that you can enjoy on 'the island of real'. The overwhelming weight of the world – 'It's too enormous' – is taken away on the island.

Several layers of vocals sing the chorus like they're sitting around a campfire, sharing the sounds of their voices and revelling in the words they sing. After the second chorus, another complex vocal arrangement – accompanied only by a lone calliope – takes over for eight bars, raising the campfire motif to a higher level. This is followed by one more half-chorus declaring plainly: 'The world is beyond us (Shit just got real)'.

Unusual for a Crowded House song, the track features a guitar solo that lasts more than six bars. It follows 12 bars of hurdy-gurdy and is positioned at the end of the song – sounding not unlike Jerry Garcia – as the island fades out into the surrounding sea.

'Sweet Tooth'

We move from a pair of songs contemplating the end of the world to a barbed allegory framed around an addiction to sugar. Finn spits out the lyrics in short spurts like his own blood sugar is running low. This short, bouncy tune plays at a tempo just right for a child to skip along to while clutching a Snickers.

The narrator is accusing someone of acting sweet when underneath, they are actually troubled and two-faced; someone who invites more people to the Chinese restaurant ('Mr Chow's') than there is enough food for; someone who teeters on the edge of decorum until they decide they've got something inappropriate to say: 'Just enough right now to put that madness in your heart'.

The chorus elaborates on how they might appear all jellybeans and lollipops on the outside but feel like they're being swallowed up by a chocolate river on the inside: 'Sweet tooth ... can't find anyone to tell your troubles to'.

When the bridge comes in after the second chorus, that's when the sugar rush really kicks in. The vocals and keyboards literally buzz with the effects of the drug, as Finn sings: 'I will never know when I've had enough. Feel it travelling in my blood ... I will never know 'til the sugars all run out'.

After the bridge, a staccato guitar solo punctuates the rush as the sugar high starts to wane. The rest of the song, arranged around the electric guitar strum and bouncy piano, is basic and catchy, settling easily into a pop pastiche.

In the end, Finn tries to see the pathology through the eyes of the addict and stops the song swiftly as he realises it might not be that person's fault: 'Don't resist it. How could anyone put that madness in your heart?'

'Whatever You Want'

In the era of Trumpism, fake news and alternative facts, songwriters and artists have not shied away from expressing their opinions. In 2017, Todd Rundgren, duetting with Donald Fagen, released 'Tin Foil Hat'; Paul McCartney had 'Despite Repeated Warnings' on his 2018 album *Egypt Station*; in 2021, Styx put out an entire concept album on the subject called *Crash Of The Crown*. And these are just some of the more cryptic ones.

Even Neil Finn couldn't resist commenting on the tumultuous waves emanating out of the White House. In 'Whatever You Want', he's chosen to focus on the sycophants who bend over backwards to satisfy their favourite megalomaniac's ego, who never call him out and enable him with their blind allegiance: 'Some will fall upon their swords in order that they might serve the greater good. But don't believe a word of it ... There are some things they will never ever say'.

The climax of the song has Finn yelling at the television, softened only by some typical Crowded House backing vocals: 'Should be shouting from the mountain at the top of their voice: This is not right, this man is a fake. But they will follow him down to the edge of the cliff and if he tells them to jump they will jump right in'. It doesn't rhyme or scan and it's not lyrical in Finn's usual style, but in this case, there are no clearer words to choose.

An instrumental break starting at 2:20 shows the bluster of these people, represented by beefy bass and saturated bottom-string guitar while they dance. This leads to the coda where choirs of angels innocently chant their truth, chosen by the Lord to spread his word, no doubt. Elroy Finn engages a 'My Sharona' (The Knack, 1979) drum beat with a snare sound that really pops through the lyrical rhetoric. Seymour's Motown-styled bass returns after a long absence, although the production has muted the tone more than usual, and Liam Finn's guitar, more aggressive than his father's, is used tastefully during fills and solos.

'Show Me The Way'

This is a country song disguised as a Crowded House song, sounding more like the old band than any of the more recent songs. Sustained guitar fills (like Hart's old lap steel), minor key chords played over a bubbling percussive groove (like 'Private Universe') and a Youth-like production sound that prefers simplicity and mood over density prevails throughout.

Lyrically, the first verse uses some well-trodden country tropes: 'When the sheriff came in my father's name' and 'I took the fall for my brother's shame'. The first pre-chorus takes it further: 'When I see red I put a handgun under my pillow'. The character in this song is cornered – by love, by the law and by his own insecurities. He wants to do the right thing, as all Western heroes do, but he reaches out in a kind of prayer for guidance, singing, 'Please show me the way to help. Show me the way to love you for real'. A choir of jolly voices singing 'doo-doo-doo' sounds distinctly out of place as we head towards the chorus.

The second verse uses a more sinister theme to engage with this prayer, referring to unwanted visitors 'with the burning cross'. This is followed by one of Finn's most cynical references to God: 'You'll forget me not when you wipe away all the holy pain'. This statement leaves the character (probably a different one from the first verse) feeling powerless and hopeless despite his unshakable faith and willingness to follow his god's will.

The coda features Finn speaking directly to the object of his prayer, intimately and vulnerably: 'Show me now, 'cause I'm still learning, it's all or nothing'.

'Goodnight Everyone' (Liam Finn)

This is the opposite of the previous track – a Crowded House song disguised as a country song. The tone and arrangement could be from a Sergio Leone film with a soundtrack by Ennio Morricone: strummed guitar, slide guitar, prancing bass lines, echoing voices and soaring strings. The instrumentation at end of the song suggests the hero is galloping off into the sunset.

However, lyrically, it's more of a mythical story. A loner, unhappy with being the centre of attention, walks away from everything he knows: 'I'm all done with fame 'cause I'm always on guard'. He says 'goodnight everyone' for the last time and goes searching for his sister. In Greek mythology, the brother and sister of Orestes and Electra team up after years apart to avenge the murder of their father, Agamemnon, by their mother, Clytemnestra. They feel such a connection to each other that when Electra finds her brother's hair and footprints near their father's grave, she feels as if they are her own. In 'Goodnight Everyone', the narrator pines to return to the warmth of his beloved sibling: 'Where are you now my sister? Wilding hair beneath the half moon. Arrange the heavens Electra'. At the end of the chorus, he implies that perhaps they might join together in some act of revenge: 'Your flaming arrow in the dawn'.

The opening line – 'Oldest form of revenue' – could refer to what is traditionally known as the world's oldest profession – prostitution. It could also mean the selling of alcohol, as the next line suggests: 'One more drink for the road'. Or, assuming the narrator is a musician – 'Those dreamless nights on the road' – it could be referring to wandering minstrels.

'Goodnight Everyone' is the first Crowded House song to be solely attributed to a songwriter other than Neil Finn since Paul Hester's 'Skin Feeling' on *Together Alone*. Liam's lead vocal clearly proves that the Finn apple doesn't fall far from the tree. The production is dense but not muddy; each instrument holds its own, sounding very much like classic Crowded House. It stands as one of the highlights of the album.

'Too Good For This World' (Neil Finn/Tim Finn)

This is a rare, latter-day Finn Brothers collaboration that recounts the dark story of a sailor's death through the album's most sing-along-able chorus. The song skims over the waves like a sea shanty, relying on acoustic instruments – mainly guitar, percussion and what sounds like a ukulele. Brushes on the snare provide a persistent resonance like a boat's bow splitting the waves.

Evidence suggests this song was inspired by the death of New Zealand champion yachtsman Sir Peter Blake (not to be confused with the British pop artist of the same name). Winner of several major sailing races, including the Whitbread Round the World race and the America's Cup, Blake later went on to lead environmental expeditions in Antarctica and the Amazon. In December 2001, his ship was raided by pirates and Blake was killed. A few weeks later, Neil and Tim Finn played the Split Enz song 'Six Months In A Leaky Boat' at Blake's memorial in Auckland.

The lyrics of 'Too Good For This World' are told from the two perspectives of an angel distraught at having to leave this mortal coil and of the ship that he sailed. 'Look at you chief, your wings are magnificent ... I may never see sailor again', the ship laments. The angel speaks to anyone who will listen:

'If you see her, tell her I love her. Maybe one day it will all make sense'. The second verse quotes the earlier song, 'To The Island': 'My sailor, my island, my dream', the ship sings. The angel echoes: 'She was just the right size for me'. The bridge encapsulates the sailor's thoughts as he reflects on his life: 'I gave myself to love ... but I only made things worse. And goodness is a curse. I must be too good for this world'.

There's an awkward moment in the second verse on the lyric, 'We made heavenly love'. It sounds like a Tim Finn line that Neil was less enthusiastic about singing. How intimate was this relationship between the captain and his ship? As a result, his delivery of the line is thrown away, nearly indistinguishable.

'Start Of Something' (Liam Finn/Neil Finn)

A breakup song that clings to the old adage 'When one door closes, another one opens', this was co-written by father and son, as they both share the vocal duties from start to finish. This is reminiscent of the Finn brothers vocal performance on *Woodface*'s 'It's Only Natural' – with which it also shares a tempo – and provides a satisfying familial continuity to the Crowded House legacy.

The news has hit the narrator hard at the start of the song – he's already knocked down: 'I'm in the ambulance. Where's the rapture, a sign to carry on?' But he soon gains some perspective on life and love: 'Walking out on you, the only one I love ... and though they tell you it's the end, it's the start of something'.

To emphasise the sense of promise, the song's tonal centre shifts from a gloomy C# minor in the verse to a buoyant E major – the relative major (which shares the same notes but has a brighter tonality) – in the chorus. The second chorus modulates to a C major key centre via passing chords, which curiously brightens up the mood even further despite it being a major third down from the E major. It's a good trick.

'Real Life Woman'

Finn connects with his bluesy side here on a song about a good woman gone bad. He also engages the rarely used John Lennon half of his Beatles melody tool kit. But overall, this song falls short. The melody is flat, the metre awkward, the rhythm and tempo plodding and it stands out as one of the few misfires in the Crowded House discography.

The lyrics are disjointed and are sung dismissively. The narrative never seems to coalesce. The song starts off describing a person who has turned to crime and cut ties with the narrator, with whom they were once involved, musically: 'I could feel your power when we were singing lines together'. He is, perhaps, her Svengali but she uses her status for her personal gain.

The chorus works on its own but is forced into double duty trying to tie the song together. It's a section of bluesy attitude – 'Talking 'bout a real life woman' – and half-rhymes – 'Every misadventure is a kind of redemption' – and overly relies on the resolution of suspended chords to create any kind of musical relief.

There is a nice vocal break after the second chorus that mercifully disengages with the clunky story for eight bars. Smooth, soaring harmonies are a welcome distraction from the rest of the lacklustre song, if only briefly.

'Love Isn't Hard At All' (Elroy Finn/Neil Finn)
The number two son gets his opportunity to share credits with the old man on this song. Sounding like a cousin of The Cure, 'Love Isn't Hard At All' could have been a hit in the 1980s, which would be older than Elroy. The layers of keyboard parts with a lone guitar figure act as an intro and also link the sections.

It's a love song that does what it says on the tin: it's joyous, immediate and feels like it's the easiest thing in the world, even if the object of the narrator's love isn't always as attentive as he is. 'Let's go, the world awaits' – it begins happily, setting the tone for an adventure. Though there is doubt: 'Those eyes are miles away … where are you?' – unrequited love is still love. The chorus proclaims, 'And in the dark I hear the call. It feels like love isn't hard at all', in one of the most celebratory lines ever sung on a Crowded House recording.

At 1:38, there is a short instrumental break which claims to quote the theme music to the popular computer game *Tetris*. That theme itself was taken from the Russian folk tune *Korobeiniki* (The Peddlers), which tells the story of a boy and girl's flirtations as they haggle for the sale of some goods. The musical reference is oblique and probably wouldn't be noticed unless you knew it was there.

About six months after the release of *Dreamers Are Waiting*, a video to this song was released focusing exclusively on American surfer Kelly Slater in action. The bridge lyrics, in particular, are very surfer-like:

> A man works hard to find his shape
> Knowing where he stands
> And how much of this he can take
> The song the siren's make
> Getting loud as the swell's about to break

All of the lead vocals are triple-tracked in unison but panned left, right and centre. The texture of the voices adds to that 1980s feel. It's a great groove but the song ends rather too abruptly.

'Deeper Down'
It seems appropriate that the first album by the new Crowded House should close out with a song that reflects Neil Finn's steadfast commitment to songwriting. Since he first showed signs of being more than just Tim

Finn's little brother in Split Enz, with songs like 'Message To My Girl', Neil wanted to show that he could dig a little deeper with poems set to music. As good artists do, he aimed to reach the depths of his mind and soul as he simultaneously discovered ways of articulating those deep dives: 'I am never one to wallow. I leapt into the ocean, went diving deeper down', he sings.

In 'Deeper Down', he also passes the torch to his sons, who have not only joined him in his musical journey but have proven themselves worthy of his wisdom. He recognises this continuity – 'A young man dim and callow, he's stolen all my clothes' – and he encourages them to explore their own depths as he did: 'Devils must be dancing in the mind of every man. Let's go deeper down'.

Finn sings in the chorus, 'I'm always reaching out for love a little deeper down' – love of a woman, of family, of music and of life. It sounds so simple coming from him; like McCartney, he sings about love like it's a shopping list.

By the time he gets to the bridge, he's made it as clear as he possibly can, writing one of the most beautiful lyrics he's managed in 40 years of writing songs: 'Like any flower on earth, from the moment of my birth, my desire is to open up'. He accentuates this feeling of opening by moving from a minor chord to a D7sus4 and resolving on D major on the word 'open'. It's a major moment that could have been even more powerful with some heightened dynamic energy.

The melody is joyous but also a bit cautious as if we should be warned not to get too carried away with our navel-gazing. Finn nearly whispers his falsetto vocal over a gentle guitar strum, simple bass line, piano, soft drumming and guitar fills.

Gravity Stairs (2024)

Personnel
Neil Finn: guitar, piano, keyboards, lead and backing vocals
Nick Seymour: bass, backing vocals
Liam Finn: guitar, keyboards, lead and backing vocals
Elroy Finn: drums, guitar, keyboards, backing vocals
Mitchell Froom: keyboards
Additional musicians
Sharon Finn: backing vocals
Tim Finn: additional vocals
Paul Taylor: percussion
Steven Schram: guitar
Ladyhawke: backing vocals
Lauryn Canny: backing vocals
Eliza-Jane Barnes: backing vocals
Jimmy Metherell: backing vocals
Zoe Moon: backing vocals
Elias Dendias: bouzouki
Antonis Moriatis: bouzouki
Nassos Vlachos: guitar
Tryfon Baitsis: guitar
Producer: Crowded House and Steven Schram
Engineer: Crowded House and Steven Schram
Mixer: Steven Schram
Recorded at Music Farm Studios (Australia), La La Mansion Studio (LA), Roundhead Studio (NZ), Studio La Fabrique (France) and Elroy's Apartment (LA)
Released on 31 May 2024 on BMG
Running time: 40:43
Highest chart position: n/a
All songs by Neil Finn, unless otherwise specified

Neil Finn, at the time of recording *Gravity Stairs*, was in his mid-sixties, almost 40 years on from the first Crowded House album and approaching 50 since he joined Split Enz. So, what keeps him focused on continuing to make music? He answered that question in the 2023 Zoom conversation:

> I'm more compelled than ever. It doesn't get any easier. But I'm prepared to put the time and energy into it. The fascination of it has just increased. If I find a new set of chords with a melody attached that has never come forward before, that's very exciting. So I'll chase that down as much as I can. An artist like Van Morrison perhaps – I don't mean to pick him out – has a familiar palette and, to a greater or lesser extent, creates records based on that same palette every time. But I'm just not that sort of guy. I'm kind of looking to find my place, and my place is shifting all the time. I sometimes

> look back and think I could've made a simpler palette for this record and it would have made it easier. It's kind of stumbling along but with a great sense of purpose and deliberation. Sometimes, you have to convince yourself it's the most important thing in the world; otherwise, you'll never get it done.

On first listen, *Gravity Stairs* sounds very much like *Dreamers Are Waiting* Part 2. This is largely a result of the same musicians – who have now played together as a unit for over four years – continuing their collective journey. Furthermore, the band's palette (as Neil Finn has referred to it) of sounds, textures, melodies and arrangements is clearly producing the same colours. These melodies share similar motifs with *Dreamers Are Waiting,* fit into the chords in the same fashion and equally cater to Finn's voice as he embraces his mature sound. Gone are the days of unpredictable vocal intervals of sixths and sevenths, lilting falsettos or screaming codas.

Further listening, however, confirms something much different. The melodies are more fluid but also less predictable. Despite Finn's penchant for writing primarily vertical melodies, here he has delivered a collection of melodies far more horizontal than any earlier album. The lyrics are denser and harder to penetrate, with more opportunities for questions and interpretation.

There are no runaway smash hits here, no rousing singalong choruses like 'Weather With You'. Rafts of hooky melodies, common to most Crowded House albums, are replaced by new sonic adventures and textures created by guitars and voices that lead these songs through completely different kinds of musical landscapes. Overall, the songwriting is more sophisticated than *Dreamers Are Waiting*. To be fair, no two Crowded House albums really sound the same.

Finn elaborated on the new sound in a 2024 interview on the YouTube channel *Kyle Meredith With...*:

> It's got a dreamy, psychedelic quality to it, which comes in largely because all of the players – certainly my son, Liam, and Mitchell – have got an approach where textures are as important as melodies and as important as chords. So we try and make a sound that is the sum total of our personalities. For me, I look forward to hearing what they're going to do with my demos. Sometimes, they're not what I expected and, generally speaking, I love to see them expand and develop character and atmosphere.

For any fan of the band, this is a good album. But if there is one thing holding *Gravity Stairs* back from being a great album, it's the production. Many layers of mid-range instrumentation and a great deal too much reverb muddy up the arrangements. A few of the songs give Seymour the opportunity to contribute some of his most interesting lines since *Time On Earth*, but his bass is often muted amid the jungle of instrumentation. None of these factors do any favours for Neil Finn's ageing voice, which naturally has decreased in range and power. Although he can still carry a song with his natural warm tone, his lower range gets lost in the arrangement, even when his vocals are double-tracked. In the earlier days of Crowded House, Finn frequently sang in full voice at the top of his register, allowing it to rise above the arrangement and cut through the mix. Consider the now iconic 'Hey now, hey now' refrain from 'Don't Dream It's Over', which sits on top of everything else even before Finn's beautiful falsetto sings the title line. But in these newer songs, the frequency of his voice is right in the middle of everything, squashed between ambient keyboards, guitar layers and thick background vocals.

Many of the production issues could be due to the nature of the recording process. Like *Dreamers Are Waiting*, this album had all the musicians contributing their parts from their disparate home locations: Neil Finn is still based in New Zealand, Seymour in Ireland, Elroy Finn in London and Liam Finn and Froom are in California. However, Finn explained to Stu Whiffen in the *Off The Beat And Track* podcast in 2024:

> We managed to gather for three periods of time in order to make the rhythm tracks of the record. First in Byron Bay, Australia, just before an Australian tour. Then, in Los Angeles, just at the end of a tour. Then, at my studio in Auckland. So those three sessions – combined with a whole lot of work at home in my private space, reworking, analysing, throwing things up in the air and rebuilding them – led to a really excellent result. And a lot of file sharing – it's the modern way. But it's been a long process.

In that scenario, there is always the tendency to add more – to make up for any collaborative discoveries – rather than leave space. These songs could benefit from a bit more space.

What hasn't changed is Finn's forensic attention to melody and especially its relationship with a lyric. In the same *Kyle Meredith With...* interview, Finn said:

> The words have to behave in a melodic way. But then there's a moment of revelation occasionally where you go, 'Oh my god, I just realised what he's singing about'. I love that process of a slow release because if music is too reliant on lyrics, you feel like you have to concentrate on it in an academic way. That's not what music is to me.

He spoke in more detail about this during the 2023 Zoom conversation.

> Endurance is just part of the process for me now. I don't know if anybody else spends that much time trying to get melodies to sit right and the words to support them. I very seldom sit down with a message that I want to get

across and then try and discover a melody to fit it. I'm normally finding words in the process that seem to support the melody and give it emotional heft. Then I just have to chase those words down and that's sometimes an agonising process because the first words you get always fit so well. Then you have to try to figure out what the hell they mean. So, I'll sacrifice a bit of meaning for a line that just puts your head in the right place.

I make assumptions sometimes about the people who I really admire. And I've been reassured to see Leonard Cohen – who I regard as one of the best lyricists in music – on record saying he'd spend a year on a lyric, moving things around, getting the right verse to go in the right place. And I think, what differentiates people that do great work? I think there are people who are like shooting stars when they're young. It always flows out of them and it must feel like it's all easy and effortless. Then, at a certain point, the chickens come home to roost and then they can't keep doing that anymore. The ones that differentiate and go on and continue to create bodies of work usually are prepared to work very hard on their craft and hopefully don't go mad in the process.

'Magic Piano'

Track one opens with a quirky but somehow familiar mechanical noise, reminiscent of 'It's Only Natural', to remind us that this band will always be singularly recognisable despite being willing to push the sonic boat out. There are some instant clues that this is still Crowded House, such as the major/minor relationship. The dreamy major key centre gets temporarily shoved aside for the contemplative minor section at the end of the verse: 'Here am I so bright, here am I so light'.

This lyric captures a moment in time, reflecting on the sensation of trying to reach a destination while peripherally, the sounds of a distant piano, a racing car and thoughts of a loved one can be a distraction. It refers directly to the gravity stairs of the album's title, as Finn explained to *Sunday Brunch* on Channel 4, UK, in 2024:

> There's a place we go to in Greece for a holiday and there are these steps that just seem to have an unusual amount of weight underneath them and it's often because we're coming home at one o'clock. It's the last slog. So they became known as the gravity stairs. We've lugged suitcases up there a few times. But, you know, that alone wouldn't have been a reason to have it. It's more about the way you've got to work a bit harder to get to the top of the stairs to achieve things, so it was a good metaphor as well.

'Teenage Summer'

The second single released from *Gravity Stairs* is driven by a strumming acoustic guitar with a double-time feel. Some lovely bass playing from Seymour through the intro and early on is eventually drowned out by an overpowering synth bass. The driving rhythm is interrupted for a short, eight-bar psychedelic bridge that does little to enhance the song or the narrative.

As the title suggests, the song harkens back to California beach songs from the early seventies from artists like America or Loggins & Messina. It even shares some lyrical similarities with the era, including the not-so-subtle: 'Baby come on. Wanted to hear you. Want to be near you'.

Steel guitar comes in at the first chorus to add some delightful texture. Afterwards, it either disappears in favour of other rhythm guitar parts or is buried too deep in the mix to notice. The overall groove is in double time but with anticipated alternating snare shots, giving it a unique groove among Crowded House songs. That said, it also prevents it from driving steadily forward, instead giving it more of a stop-and-start feel.

Originally listed as 'Life's Imitation', the title was changed to 'Teenage Summer' a few weeks before release.

'The Howl' (Liam Finn)

Moving at a 'Locked Out' tempo but with less muscle, Liam Finn's contribution is a cryptic song that includes references to a sword-swinging sorceress, Groundhog Day and some disembodied narrator who howls like a werewolf. Some metaphorical lyrics, such as 'Underwater I'm the land', don't quite work and the repetitive melody does little to help bring order to the seemingly random words.

The narrator seems to be working toward the payoff of the final line, 'I've held my breath so far. I shake my body up. And I will howl', but there is no dynamic shift or change in intensity to the arrangement to give this howl much power. Considering all the similarities between Liam's and Neil's voices, Liam lacks his father's vocal earnestness.

For a song this fast – about 128 bpm – the drums are mixed very quietly and fail to bolster the rest of the rhythm section. Instead, it relies on guitar interplay – one steady acoustic and up to three electric – for its momentum.

'All That I Can Ever Own'

Without a doubt the sweetest song on *Gravity Stairs*, 'All That I Can Ever Own' harkens back to old-school Neil Finn writing about love in 'Into Temptation' or 'Fall At Your Feet' (with which it shares a groove). Finn reflects on his time on earth, his age (he's a grandfather now) and the important people in his life. There can be little doubt about the sentiment expressed in: 'As I grow old, I'm grateful. When I hold this child in my arms, heaven knows I'm hopeful'.

With these reflections, he discovers '...on the ride home, that when love is in my heart, it's all that I can ever own'. He shows how he'll do anything to protect that love: 'And my worries keep me awake', he sings. Even, as he so often does, invoking God as both mysterious spirit and guardian: 'Someone is waiting, maybe a stranger. One day he'll guide you home'.

This arrangement is simple and straightforward, effectively using backing vocals, sparse guitar fills and very little piano. It packs a big punch in just over three minutes.

'Oh Hi'

For the album's first single, the band chose this song inspired by, as Finn told *Kyle Meredith With ...*, the uplifting story of school children in small African villages:

> This song existed before that connection was made. I was looking for a lyrical thread on it and I started talking to this woman who runs an organisation called So They Can – I've been supporting them for many years – who have been helping build and resource schools and other facilities in Kenya and Tanzania in quite remote and economically depressed areas. It's been a really amazing success story. So she asked if I would write a song for these kids and this song happened to present itself. And the words became influenced by that. I was intent on making the song stand on its own legs without anyone knowing the backstory, but it was created for and inspired by these kids.

The impetus for writing such uplifting lines as 'Every child is a mystic, having visions of a new dawn. Be the one in a million that could lift the sun' is clear. The title lyric in the chorus of 'Oh Hi' is sung like a little wave of greeting to the children in that African village as if to say he can see them, hoping to remind them that they have the potential to reach out and affect the whole world. In turn, he is saying we all can.

One of the simpler arrangements on the album, this song is carried by the singalong chorus, complete with a choir of voices representing the children. The soft pop sound meshes with the linear melody and then takes a dynamic break in the bridge as Finn sings, 'There's something wrong with the state of my head, but I know you can get to the heart of it', before resuming the guitar strumming groove. Five times throughout, the arrangement is punctuated by a jarring electric descending trill that's more distracting than colourful.

'Some Greater Plan (For Claire)' (Neil Finn/Tim Finn)

A tremulous pair of bouzoukis opens this loping 6/8 number, which trundles along like a sleepy country song of longing with a Mediterranean feel. Quietly plaintive steel guitar blankets the background, along with heavily echoing background vocals. It could be a John Hiatt or Roy Orbison song. Elroy Finn's brushed drums are soft and steady, appropriately applying a folksy flavour to the groove. But one can't help but wonder how Paul Hester's inimitable brush strokes might have added a bit more punch to this song.

The Finns often spoke about how their mother's values and religious influences had seeped into their music, but for the first time, their father makes an appearance. The 'Claire' of the title had been mentioned in 'the World War II diaries of Dick Finn, Neil and Tim's father', as Neil told John Aizlewood in the June 2024 issue of *Mojo*:

> He sneaked into an officers' dance in Florence. He met this diplomat's daughter and they had a wonderful two-week affair. When he came home, he met my mum. They had a beautiful, happy marriage but he always had a wistful look when he talked about Italy. It became a family joke.

What seems to start as a song where our narrator is trying to bolster the confidence in the object of his affection – 'Your life is just beginning, the war it never ends ... you are gorgeous and absurd' – ends with a rather more deferential voice saying, 'I'm there if you want to be a part of some greater plan', before finally descending into desperation, asking her, 'do you want to heal the heart of this broken man?' This transition happens slowly and with subtlety and the lyrics are offered in sparse bursts of thought as the strumming, twangy guitar continues throughout.

The main dynamic shift occurs in the chorus when Finn sings over a minor-key passage – 'If all that we can do is fill the room' – before resolving, in typical Finn fashion, on the major chord as he sings, 'With a song of love'.

'Black Water, White Circle'

With the most interesting musical introduction on the album – a polyrhythmic interplay between arpeggiated guitar, some airy keyboard and percussion – that launches into a captivating cha-cha, this song makes a big promise from the top. But the Latin feel is quickly washed away by keyboard pads, guitar fills and voices thick with reverb. Froom's colourful piano trills are buried by the other instruments and, in the second verse, far too prominent backing vocals. Toward the end, even the multi-tracked lead vocals get drowned out.

The real strength of 'Black Water, White Circle' is its lyric, sounding like old-school Neil Finn. It's a moment in time by the lakeside at night with the reflecting moon, where the narrator is as captivated with the view as he is by his lover: 'The willow bending, the flame ascending. Our love consenting to go further'. He is sharing it with her and also using its beauty as a metaphor for her own: 'Luminescent eyes that look out of the incoming waves tonight my love'. Later, in the bridge, he confesses, 'She is the force that leads me to the lake on the day of the dead', referring to the annual Mexican celebration of lost loved ones. This not only thematically ties the lyric and music together but also suggests that the lover he is sharing the night with has already passed away. A Finnian twist like no other.

'Blurry Grass' (Neil Finn/Elroy Finn)

Sounding like Beck in one of his retro moods, 'Blurry Grass' is arguably the catchiest song on *Gravity Stairs*. It's also one of the best-sounding recordings on the album, with a crisp mix that doesn't blur the lines as much between instruments. Seymour's wandering bass sounds as free and happy-go-lucky as it has since *Intriguer*. The vocals still have too much reverb but are otherwise present and upfront. Irish actress Lauryn Canny's background vocals, sounding appropriately like Sandy Denny, complete the song's throwback sound.

The lyrics are a bit harder to penetrate. The blurry grass of the title appears to be where this narrator has found himself after a particularly bad trip. What generated this result is not exactly clear: 'Am I ever gonna get that thought from my bed? You say it's passion, what you'd imagine, you've seen a ghost'. All we really know is that he 'woke up on the lawn covered in bugs and butterflies'.

At the 1.30 mark, there is a quiet psychedelic break that evolves into a short guitar solo with vocals doubling the melody. The vocal refrain of 'on the blurry grass…' at the beginning of the song and at the outro sounds like an ambulance siren sent to rescue this prostrate character.

'I Can't Keep Up With You' (Neil Finn/Liam Finn)

A solid metaphor about never quite feeling good enough – 'Riding on the roundabout, I am bound to follow you now. I can hardly catch up from behind' – starts this one off before the arrival of a catchy chorus. Gradually, the focus of the lyric changes from inadequacy to admiration: 'And suddenly you're irresistible. They compare you to the poet Byron'. By the time the second bridge comes in – sounding like a children's taunting chorus – it's become positively surreal: 'Show me something good again. A case of wine, ich liebe dich. It's awkward at the start, then we saw the animals'.

The arrangement skips along like 'Chocolate Cake', pulling you along by the hand until you discover what it's about. It shares a groove with U2's 'Zoo Station' and includes a similarly fashioned distorted guitar. Liam Finn's guitar fills are used judiciously but effectively in the left and right channels, highlighting the rhythm guitar in the centre. With all that's going on in the energetic arrangement, the vocals seem to lack energy by comparison.

The musical directness balances out the oblique lyrics and makes this one of the more enjoyable listens on *Gravity Stairs*. Listen out for the cartoonish, Python-esque background vocals that start around 2:25.

'Thirsty' (Neil Finn/Elroy Finn)

As Neil Finn continues to explore uncommon song forms, this one uses the almost impossible A B A B C D E. The catchy refrain – 'How come some people never get thirsty' – is sung twice in the first half of the song and then never again in the second half.

It's a silly love song – Neil's lyric set to Elroy's music – that features some of Finn's finest poetry on the album: 'When love comes early, handsome, burly, looks you in the eye. I saw a sea burning and the earth linger in a timeless dream'. It's about seizing the day (or, in this case, the night) because the constant quest to enjoy life is unquenchable. 'Don't dilly dally', he sings, 'don't delay fun'.

By far the simplest arrangement on *Gravity Stairs,* 'Thirsty' is more of a musical throwback to classic Crowded House. It's made up of softly played acoustic guitars (at least two, maybe three), bass, brushed snare, sparing electric guitar fills and minor use of string pads from the keyboard. This gives Finn's voice ample space to manoeuvre and allows for some colourful backing vocals.

'Night Song'

One of the most unusual songs ever to have been included on a Crowded House album, both in form and melodically, 'Night Song' is an odd choice as a closer. A song in three movements, it starts as a quiet waltz (evocative of other 3/4 time album closers: 'How Will You Go', 'Time Immemorial' and 'Elephants') led by piano and bass. This section's lyric is a simple plea to whisk someone away on an adventure.

The second movement, a mere 16 bars starting at 1:51, evolves into a 4/4 swing still arranged around the piano and bass but with some more percussion and a swirling soundscape from Finn's Prophet synth keyboard. Here, Finn sings about the regret of missing out on the adventure from the first movement: 'Remembering you got me so inspired. Felt so lonely when I passed your gate, round the corner, by then it's too late'.

The final section – which has its own A B A A form – has a more straightforward groove, so much so that when the snare jarringly kicks in, it sounds as close to hip-hop as Crowded House would ever dare to go. It features a short vibraphone solo and only one discernible guitar track. The night song of the title comes to Finn, as with many songwriters, as if in a dream: 'Here it comes, another night song stuck in my brain. Wish there was another way'.

When asked about the different movements on *Kyle Meredith With...* in 2024, Finn described them all coming from an experimental expedition on the Prophet:

> It's a to-be-continued kind of thing. I've got some nice pieces that follow it up, all deriving from the same wonky Prophet sound – you might hear it in there. It's common to all three pieces. So I'm going to explore that; it would be kind of fun to start the next record with a 15-minute continuation of that jam.

Extra Songs

In November 2016, Capitol/Universal released Deluxe Editions of the first seven Crowded House studio albums, including *Afterglow*. They included live performances, demos of their recognisable songs, B-sides and some never-before-heard recordings. With some notable exceptions, many of these songs were quite rightly left off any major release. It can be easy for listeners and fans of any artist to forget the amount of work put into every recording, which could result in many hours of tape being tossed out. Sometimes, questionable recordings are released to keep fans happy regardless of their quality.

Having said that, the Crowded House legacy may very well be the absence of many clunkers. Finn and company's output remained high in quality for nearly 40 years, so perhaps space can be made to allow for a few songs that missed the target.

Included in this section are completed songs that appeared on deluxe issues, studio demos/rough mixes of songs that sound complete and a few live recordings of complete songs not released anywhere else. Not included here are home demos, live versions of album tracks, alternate studio versions, partial or incomplete songs, repurposed Split Enz songs, Neil Finn solo recordings or songs that evolved into later-released songs (e.g. 'Creek Song'/'Left Hand').

They are listed here chronologically (that album's Deluxe Edition in parentheses). Personnel will be consistent with the year of the session in which each song was recorded.

All songs by Neil Finn unless otherwise specified.

'Walking On The Pier' (Crowded House)

This features a dour, despondent lyric set to a happy-go-lucky beat. The narrator, while walking on an actual pier, dreams of being anywhere other than where he is: 'Transplanted my body ... to this godforsaken country, to this monumental hole'. A bit of an Angry Young Man moment for Finn.

Unusually, there are only A and B sections. The two sections, only a tone apart, move awkwardly between each other as Finn's unoriginal melody does little to showcase his songwriting abilities.

'Does Anyone Here Understand My Girlfriend' (Paul Hester) (Crowded House)

Most notable about this Hester song is his energetic drumming. His popping snare, rim shots and hi-hat work sound like vintage Stewart Copeland. Coupled with some imaginative bass fills by Seymour, this song fits in nicely with the post-punk pop of the early 1980s.

The lyric refers to the famous 1947 photograph of Evelyn McHale lying on the crumpled roof of a car after jumping from the 86th-floor observation deck of the Empire State Building in New York City.

'Oblivion' (Crowded House)
The Angry Young Man rides again in this tale of feeling lost and abandoned in faraway New Zealand: 'We are out of the way, heading for oblivion, easy to isolate'. Dynamically unvaried, it's missing the memorable hook found in every song from the first album. Nevertheless, the musicianship is excellent. Finn has been quoted as saying it nearly made the cut, but realistically, it would have been heavily overshadowed by the rest of the first album's material.

'Burnt Out Tree' (Temple Of Low Men)
At barely a minute and a half long, it reads like a quick sermon on the mount about admitting your sins now and being blessed later: 'There's only one way to play this game, but the rules are not written and it has no name'.

This live performance, though apparently a complete thought – an earlier home demo is identical – would almost certainly have segued into another song.

'My Legs Are Gone' (Woodface)
A really strong chorus – 'Caught on a bad day, caught on a bad day. I don't know which side I'm on' – can't make up for this fragmented song about drinking too much. Many of the verse lyrics don't fit the music, despite Finn's best efforts.

The final minute is a very listenable instrumental bad trip, played out with phased guitars and xylophone.

'Fields Are Full Of Your Kind' (Woodface)
A solid lyric devoted to the memory of fallen soldiers, effective lines include, 'And my dreams are covered in red. And I know this is happening to me'. The song's undoing lies in Finn's penchant for writing minor chord verses and major chord choruses. The haunting verses turn happy too quickly for the sentiment of remembrance. Otherwise, it could have been a good fit for *Woodface*.

There's a lovely, emotive performance by Seymour throughout and especially during the bridge starting at 1.50 – 'And the flowers are in bloom'. There are nice harmonies in this production, complete with an army band (played on the keyboard) interlude starting at 2:06. The song ends strongly with powerful descending chords reminiscent of 'Mansion In The Slums'.

'Tail Of A Comet' (Together Alone)
This polished and energetic live recording of the unreleased song suggests it was ready to present to the world, but it doesn't quite live up to the standard recognised during this era of Crowded House. The lyric seems to play on the elation felt while high – either naturally or otherwise – but it doesn't really go anywhere.

The chorus is stronger than the verse and might have worked with some artistic input in the studio.

'Newcastle Jam' (Neil Finn/Paul Hester/Mark Hart/Nick Seymour) (Together Alone)
Crowded House channel Aerosmith in this guitar-heavy song born from an on-stage jam in Newcastle, Australia. Two guitars stand firm above a 'Sweet Emotion' bassline, overdubbed organ and solid drums. Finn is quoted in the 2016 Deluxe Edition:

> I remember that show being an especially good Crowded House show. Just a top night in part because we'd been for a swim at the beach in Newcastle. I always thought that that's a fantastic thing to do before you go on stage – to all take a swim in the ocean together.

The resulting song – about a tough guy who couldn't tame his lifestyle until it was too late – sounds very much like a work in progress. If Finn's melodies are usually memorable, this song proves that they don't come without a lot of work.

'Convent Girls' (Together Alone)
This is a creepy song whose narrator discusses pining for girls who are not within his reach for various reasons: 'And the convent girls in their frilly white tights. And the chorus girls with their names up in lights … I'll build a shrine within my mind, to their image I will succumb.'

Seymour's quasi-'Whispers And Moans' bassline anchors this groove, which is otherwise unremarkable. It's a cohesive song, but it would have been completely out of place on *Together Alone*.

'Zen Roxy' (Neil Finn/Mark Hart/Paul Hester/Nick Seymour) (Together Alone)
This is a piece of instrumental music released with the 'Nails In My Feet' single in November 1993. It's nearly seven minutes of aquatic psychedelia, complete with wave sounds, bongos and Hawaiian lap steel. It's not an entirely unpleasant listen; after about four minutes, you can imagine it used as a soundtrack in a documentary about New Zealand wildlife.

According to neilfinn.com: 'Legend has it that 'Zen Roxy' was mixed according to the late-night rule of having only four faders up on the desk at one time. No lyrics were ever written for the song'.

'Anthem' (Afterglow)
Set at a 'Fall At Your Feet' tempo, 'Anthem' is arguably the strongest song never issued on a major Crowded House album. It could have been a huge hit if released at a more strategic time.

The sentiment Finn sings is heart-warming and genuine: 'There for my children. There for my woman ... I'm humming to myself, my own anthem'. They are his whole world, a nation of their own with an anthem to sing in joyous patriotism. It's a song he sings to drown out the sound of his debilitating weaknesses that could jeopardise his happiness.

The chorus builds chromatically to set up a bridge that bolsters his resolve even though he might be separated from those he loves: 'And I come to my senses just before I close the door. And I won't be kept apart from the ones that I adore'. A short interlude offers an international flavour with Middle Eastern voices and strings.

As the song continues, we learn there might be a fracture in this narrator's family: 'A prayer in the silence. Think of forgiveness, an end to the violence'. But the family song, their anthem, he hopes, will keep them together as he pleads for them to 'keep it in your mind'.

'Anthem' is anthemic in a restrained way. The arrangement is basic and doesn't resort to bombastic orchestrations to justify its significance.

'I Don't Know You' (Mark Hart) (Afterglow)

This is the only song credited solely to Mark Hart in the entire discography and it doesn't quite fit in. It sounds like efforts were made for it to sound like a Crowded House song; the interplay between the two guitars and bass is classic *Together Alone*-era Finn-Hart-Seymour, and the chorus – 'I don't know you like I thought I did' – could have come straight from Finn. But it's dynamically flat and Hart's lead vocal doesn't meet the standard set by Finn's warm tones.

A more polished version of the song was released on Hart's 2001 solo album *Nada Sonata*.

'A Taste Of Something Divine' (Neil Finn/Nicky Seymour/Mark Hart/ Peter Jones/Paddy Free) (Afterglow)

One of the few recordings made during the drummer Peter Jones era, it also includes input from Kiwi electronic musician Paddy Free, who was featured on Finn's *Try Whistling This* album. The result, lacking the melodic hooks Finn often saved for Crowded House, sounds like it might fit on that album. Finn explained in the 2016 Deluxe Edition:

> There was a lot of electronic stuff happening at the time. As a traditional four-piece band, we were interested in that process. We jammed it a lot and then went through and sampled bits from the jam that we liked. We laid out all these samples on a keyboard and then played a structure down.

The obscure lyric that snakes through the slinky groove explores a mother/child relationship and its love/hate inclinations. It's difficult to imagine a Crowded House release where this song would have seemed a natural inclusion.

'Spirit Of The Stairs' (Afterglow)
This was inspired by the French expression *l'esprit d'escalier*, referring to the regret of not having a clever response during a heated conversation, which is only realised after the animosity has long passed: 'The spirit of the stairs. Everyone thinks, but no one dares. Wishes make a sad lament after he's gone'.

With work, the song could have been strong enough to make it onto one of two albums – *Together Alone* or *Time On Earth*, maybe – but suffers from some awkwardness between the metre of the lyric and 6/8 time signature. It ends, however, with a formidable two-minute instrumental section that features some of Finn's best electric guitar playing and builds to a satisfying climax. It's worth a closer listen.

'Here's A Note' (Time On Earth)
According to Neil Finn in the 2016 Deluxe Edition:

> The lyric is very much about my Dad, who keeps notes for everything. He'll write a little note, or he'll cut a bit of the newspaper out to remind him of something and then he'll put piles around the house. It's like a filing system for him. It's a good way of tidying your mind – writing notes to yourself.

Finn's paternal inspiration resulted in a lovely lyric about respecting people's idiosyncrasies and identifying the potential inheritance of that gene. It's told from the perspective of the father: 'I came upon a lost verse. They sent the prose to quench my thirst ... Here's a note you'll want to unfold'. And later: 'Where'd you go, my own dear son? Write it down before it's begun. Pass it on before you get old'. There are worse habits Finn could inherit from his father.

Musically, it's less inspiring. A jangly guitar drives the song hastily forward; it might work better at a slower tempo. The melody is basic and the arrangement leaves little time for the song to breathe and the lyric to be appreciated.

'Purple Light' (Time On Earth)
This is an enjoyable listen with a hooky melody and a terrific vocal performance by Finn. Created during the *Time On Earth* sessions, 'Purple Light', with its esoteric lyric and upbeat arrangement, probably didn't fit into the deeper, darker mood of that album. It has a light, bouncy groove with a typically Finn-like minor/major trajectory that adds both mystery and mirth.

It appears to be about a moment, perhaps accompanied by some drinks, when you reflect on a specific part of your life worthy of review. With some lyrical revision, this song could have made the cut on any other major Crowded House release.

'So Dramatic' (Time On Earth)
Originally released with the 'She Called Up' single, 'So Dramatic' follows the life and career of someone destined for stardom. As a child, they

played dress-up while craving attention. They grew up to become 'the main attraction, a star on your door' but quickly discovered the perils of that kind of attention: 'The clothes behind you, the shadow of doubt. A crowd of people that follow you about'. Ultimately, they are faced with the realisation, 'You'll have to make a sacrifice if you are like all the rest. A victim of your own success', all the while wearing a mask to hide their true self.

A slow, piano-based waltz with liberal use of a synthesised clarinet, it shares a mood with 'You Are The One To Make Me Cry' but lacks that song's sweet melody and expressive lyric.

'Distance Across' (Time On Earth)

Finn's website claims this was a 'distant forerunner' of 'Say That Again', but the similarities are indistinguishable. They share a few chord changes, but the feel is unrecognisable and the lyric is entirely unique.

'Distance Across' trips along with an 'Ob-La-Di, Ob-La-Da' jauntiness that easily pulls the melody along. The lyrics, sounding very much like a first draft, work around two figures further apart than they want to be: 'Find out where we're going to navigate the distance across'. Some notable lyrics include: 'Where my hell awaits is where my head awaits'.

'Lost Island' (Time On Earth)

This is a song about Finn's home life in New Zealand, feeling a million miles away from the rest of the world, with nods to his 'child' and his 'girl': 'Step on the gas, our glorious past is catching up with us ... In billowing clouds where the lost island is found'. Finn said of it on Fangradio, his online live music portal, in 2020:

> One of my favourites. It's a West Coast (New Zealand) song, looking at Lion Rock, watching the sun disappear into the little mouth at the end of the rock, full of dreams and possibilities.

It's another 6/8 song arranged around the strumming acoustic guitar. The melody is strong, but the arrangement includes some inappropriately grand choral backing vocals. It was originally included on the Australian CD single of 'Don't Stop Now'.

'Stare Me Out' (Time On Earth)

Released with the same 'Don't Stop Now' single, 'Stare Me Out' is a high-energy, double-time Motown groove cross between 'Pump It Up' (Elvis Costello) and 'Saturday Night' (Bay City Rollers), with a great use of horns. It's about a guy who doesn't mind being stared at and pitied (by lizards and praying mantises, apparently): 'I told him, do anything you want. Your life is yours to own'.

A fairly basic guitar solo by Elroy Finn looms large in Finn's memory of the recording, as he explained in the Crowded House Club newsletter in 2007:

That song is Elroy's debut as an electric guitarist, and, in fact, that very prominent solo on there is the very first played in his life. He did it on the floor, live with the rhythm track and added a little bit afterwards, so that moment means a lot to me.

'The Only Way To Go Is Forwards' (Intriguer)
Everything you need to know about this song is in the title. When you're at your lowest, reality can be a tough meal to swallow: 'Drink up before we all get shot. Old friend, I'll tell you what we've got. Not too much time before they bury us'.

Along with two other new songs released on the *Intriguer* Deluxe Edition, this live track was recorded at an Auckland concert played in preparation for the studio sessions for that album. Distinctive 'I Got You' (Split Enz) guitar stabs start this one off and the energy stays high throughout. It's the kind of song that would be difficult to capture with the same live energy in the studio.

The 'oh-oh, oh-oh-oh-oh-oh' refrain at the end is enjoyable to listen to and would surely welcome a live sing-along in concert.

'Beautiful Life' (Intriguer)
In the face of hardship, bad luck and the passage of time, Finn reminds us that little things can shed a beautiful light on us when we need it. 'It's a beautiful life. Beginning with pain, ending in sorrow ... It's a welcoming smile that arrives on time ... a pick-me-up sign ...'

Arranged around Finn's piano, there is also a nice use of melodica, adding colour to the slow groove. Matt Sherrod's drumming is notable, preferring short rolls over snare shots on beat two of most bars. There is no evidence of a studio recording of this song available to the public. Another song with no proper chorus it makes good use of an instrumental section in the final two minutes that goes on a nice journey.

'Bound To Rescue' (Intriguer)
This live version works much better than the piano-based home demo released on the *Time On Earth* Deluxe Edition. 'Bound To Rescue' has a melody that would sit right in the pocket of any Crowded House album.

It's a melancholy song that, like many of Finn's sadder ones, tries to end on an uplifting note. Like 'Fall At Your Feet', the narrator takes responsibility for hurting the feelings of his loved one and vows to make amends as gallantly as he can: 'Upon my hopes, let the battle commence. There is my honour, bound to rescue'. There is even a possible reference to Finn's wife, Sharon (middle name Dawn, as discovered in 'I Love You Dawn'): 'Dawn, he has no intellect. Any danger will with his sword protect'.

'God Lives Over The Road' (Intriguer)
This is a tedious instrumental, aside from Finn's Latin incantations summoning the Spiritus Sancti and some humming along the way. Guitar with

heavy reverb and pedal steel accompany the chanting, until an organ joins in about halfway through, along with the sound of a theremin at 2.18.

'Better Things' (Intriguer)
Electric piano leads the rhythm section in this light-hearted song about being a bumbling fool but, never mind, 'I go on to better things'. The song leaps happily through its changes and slowly builds in intensity with lap steel fills, gaining momentum with some sinister sounding r&b, including an 'I Wish' (Stevie Wonder) bass line and Billy Preston-style keyboards, over which Finn shouts, 'I intend to make my home and I never, never wait up'. Then it's back to the original groove and a slow fadeout. The entire song comes across as a first draft.

'The Intriguer' (Intriguer)
Only in Crowded House could you have an album named after a song named after a fictional character, and that song doesn't even appear on the album. Such is the intrigue of 'The Intriguer'. Finn tried to define this character to Jeremy Ansell for the Deluxe Edition:

> The Intriguer is the designer of unexpected events. He's a character that [Australian cartoonist] Michael Leunig and I invented from being in a hotel lobby in Sydney and observing some intriguing behaviour behind a curtain on the seventh floor.

He's a shadowy, Machiavellian spirit that may or may not even exist. When you insist someone is surreptitiously trying to drive you crazy, that's him. Intriguingly, while Finn's song refers to the character as female, Leunig's cartoon explanation, featured in the 2010 tour programme, describes him as male. It's a unique and charming characterisation for a song, which, to this day, continues to fascinate Finn, as he explained in the 2023 Zoom conversation:

> I really liked it. I don't know why it didn't end up on the record. I think I had trouble reconciling the words. There was something wrong with describing the Intriguer when the Intriguer begs not to be described. He is a presence in our lives, a mischief-maker who is always working around the fringes. I liked it better as an instrumental; in fact, we might have decided to do it as an instrumental, but it was battling other songs on the record. So it got left off to the side, which is intriguing in itself that the album's title track is not on the record.

The song is a delight. It's no stretch to call it an exuberant 7/4 time version of the *Sesame Street* theme song. To this quirky rhythm, Finn sings about having to give into the ghostly presence whenever faced with mysterious failings:

'Sometimes I think it's just bad luck … but then again, I suspect that someone plays a hand. It's a game. Then she loves to watch and laugh at my mistakes'.

The Intriguer is impish, as implied by the employment in the final verse of boyish 'doo-doo-doo's, whistling and glockenspiel all in unison. The narrator admits, equally playfully, 'You're never wrong. But in the end, I can't resist you'. Finally, the whole affair is played out with several good-humoured 'Hey's and hooting as a spectral female voice chants in the background, reminding you that she's always there to trip you up again.

'Turn It Around' (Intriguer)

This song comes across as a kind of mini prog rock suite, starting with some Tony Banks piano triplets, Steve Howe guitar arpeggios and drums with major play on the floor toms. It ends with an epic C minor pedal from the full band, with a euphonium solo – sounding heavily influenced by John Entwistle's French horn on The Who's *Tommy* – played by Kiwi musician and friend of the band Don McGlashan.

Finn sings lofty prog-like phrases, such as 'rescue the chord' and 'breathe on the stone, the monument always frozen', before finally crashing back down to earth with 'blame it on the drugs'. He sounds breathless as if he's in a hurry to explore this strange trip. Overall, it's another great vocal performance by Finn, his falsetto tone as clear as it has ever been. With some work on the arrangement, the song could have found a home on one of Finn's solo albums.

'Eyes Grow Heavy' (Intriguer)

This is a strange sort of lullaby that has the narrator standing guard through the night over his family and his home at the threat of intruders: 'Before they break in and steal the silver, thieves come 'round to admire the lock'.

It's the consummate Crowded House chorus, bringing the peril down to earth. He hopes he can stay awake long enough to scare the bad guys off, all the while at the bedside of a loved one: 'And when the moment comes, you won't remember this touch or anything at all'. A vocal interlude before the final chorus is the making of this song. It is a multi-part arrangement that beautifully insinuates the passing of time: a clock chiming, another hour passing.

'Two Minutes Of Silence' (Neil Finn/Mark Hart/Nick Seymour/Matt Sherrod) (Intriguer)

A soldier is alone on a mission. All he knows is that he's 'covered in blood' and taken by the 'billions of stars'. Finn's melody rings out like a deafening voice in the soldier's head. The band try to capture the sense of loneliness amid pressures most people will never know, with chiming guitar – like a dulcimer – ethereal sounds over the top, harp, minimal percussion and solo harmonies. The soldier is 'a shadow man … drifting and stumbling around'. But like most who take their orders and rely on their training, 'we live to fight another day'. Voices at the end cascade down two-and-a-half octaves in a kind of choral 'Amen'.

'Nonsense Of Course' (Neil Finn/Mark Hart/Nick Seymour/Matt Sherrod) (Intriguer)

Two songs in one – streaming platforms call it a medley, and elsewhere, the second part has been called a hidden track. In between the two songs, during a gap of about ten seconds, Neil Finn can be faintly heard muttering somewhere in the studio, 'Nonsense, of course. Just sounds, but...' This seems to be the genuine theme of these lyrics because it's essentially nine minutes of gibberish. The internet has varying versions of the words. Even Finn's own website doesn't appear to have much confidence in them.

The first part features a bottom-heavy arrangement with a hard kick and floor tom accenting the 'four-and' of every bar, and an adventurous bass line. Mandolin, pedal steel, treble percussion and many voices, including Finn screaming something about 'a cult with no leader', adorn the track.

The second part opens with galloping percussion and acoustic guitar before morphing into a Crowded House version of disco. The musicianship is great, the melody welcoming and, overall, it's a fun listen. The lyrics are hard to penetrate, but it appears to be telling a story of aliens being welcomed to Earth amid flames and lots of dancing: 'They are the strangest friends you've got', goes the hooky refrain. A more polished version appeared as 'Strangest Friends' on Finn's 2014 solo album *Dizzy Heights*.

Other Neil Finn Recordings

The recordings listed here are derived from all readily available sources. Any omissions are unintentional.

Finn – The Finn Brothers (1995)

When Neil and Tim Finn got together to write songs for a recording project in 1989, the fates convened and the result was Crowded House's third album, *Woodface*. After Tim's short-lived participation with the Crowdies and the subsequent *Together Alone* album and tour, the band started to implode. During this time, the brothers got together again and finally completed this: the first album that was theirs and theirs alone. Sounding like a pared-down Split Enz recording, Neil and Tim played all the instruments (except for one bass track). The standout songs are 'Only Talking Sense', 'Last Day Of June' and 'Suffer Never'.

Try Whistling This – Neil Finn (1998)

Arguably Finn's strongest work outside of Crowded House, these melodies reflect Finn in one of his peak songwriting periods. Released five years after *Together Alone*, many of the songs are crying out for Nick Seymour's bass feel or Paul Hester's organic drumming. Instead, there are keyboard loops and programmed sounds that push it in another sonic direction. However, Finn is in good voice throughout and it's an enjoyable listen. Highlights include 'Last One Standing', 'She Will Have Her Way', 'Sinner' and the title track.

One Nil – Neil Finn (2001)

Despite the heavy involvement of Wendy Melvoin and Lisa Coleman – two major components of Prince's 1980s band the Revolution – this is a largely acoustic, lo-fi album. It also marks the reunion of Finn and Mitchell Froom, who hadn't worked together since *Woodface* ten years earlier. This album uses a fairly narrow sonic 'palette' to use Finn's words, but the songs get better with every listen.

One Nil was reworked for the US market in 2002 as *One All*, which replaced 'Don't Ask Why' and 'Elastic Heart' with 'Lullaby Requiem' and 'Human Kindness'.

Rain – Film Soundtrack (2001)

Finn contributed instrumental music and five songs – some co-written with Edmund McWilliams – for this small New Zealand film. These songs, with sparse arrangements, tap into Finn's moody musical inclinations while also allowing space for them to fit neatly into the film. Unlike his usual lyrics, which allow him to explore vast emotional landscapes, the lyrics for these songs are more restrained as they're written for purpose. Still, 'Orange And Blue' and 'Drive Home' could fit nicely into a package with other moody Crowded House material.

7 Worlds Collide (2001 and 2009)
These were two charity projects – the first a live concert, the second a studio project – featuring Neil and several other collaborators, including Tim Finn, Eddie Vedder, Johnny Marr, Jeff Tweedy, KT Tunstall and more.

The live recording features Finn sharing the stage with various guests as he performs mostly solo work from *One Nil*. On the second recording, called *The Sun Came Out*, Finn only appears on four of the 24 tracks: 'Little By Little', written and performed with Sharon Finn; 'Learn To Crawl' with Johnny Marr, Ed O'Brien (Radiohead) and Liam Finn; 'All Comedians Suffer'; and 'Hazel Black' with KT Tunstall. The first two are decent original songs, but the last two are weaker.

Everyone Is Here – The Finn Brothers (2004)
The true highlight of this release is the one-of-a-kind brotherly vocal blend. Sadly, on this occasion, it's lost on some fairly forgettable songs. Even the participation of Mitchell Froom as producer can't rescue this bland offering. 'Nothing Wrong With You' and 'Anything Can Happen' are the best songs of the set.

Pajama Club – Pajama Club (2011)
This album is the result of Neil and Sharon Finn becoming empty nesters. The two of them alone in their music room began jamming – Neil on drums, Sharon on bass – and found themselves recording what became this album. The lyrics are cheeky and the music is adventurous, similar to artists such as Talking Heads or XTC. Start with 'Tell Me What You Want' and 'TNT For 2'.

A 2011 tour, that included Sean Donnelly and Alana Skyring as band members, was completed before the album's release. Neil Finn told *The Guardian* in 2011:

> Some people aren't gonna get it; it's not as 'songy', in a traditional way, as Crowded House ... I like what happens when you keep yourself open to new things happening. It keeps the music fresh and alive.

Song Of The Lonely Mountain – The Hobbit Soundtrack (2012)
Naturally, any song featured in a film project of this size will have input from several sources. While the lyric is credited to Finn, the entire songwriting team includes Neil Finn, David Donaldson, David Long, Steve Roche and Janet Roddick. The result is a plodding, Celtic folk ballad imbued with images of embattled wanderers. It was used for the end credits of *The Hobbit: An Unexpected Journey.*

Goin' Your Way – Neil Finn and Paul Kelly (2013)
A live recording from the short Australian tour by two Antipodean icons. It contains mainly acoustic versions of Crowded House, Neil Finn solo and Finn

Brothers songs, as well as some of Kelly's best. Finn sings beautifully on a version of Kelly's 'You Can Put Your Shoes Under My Bed'.

Dizzy Heights – Neil Finn (2014)
An unimaginative album by Finn's standards, with little sonic variety from start to finish, *Dizzy Heights* suffers from overproduction by Finn and Dave Fridmann (The Flaming Lips). The first track, 'Impressions', is a moody opener that lures the listener in, only to fall steeply downhill from there. The title track sounds like a forgettable deep cut from Kool And The Gang. 'Better Than TV' and 'Pony Ride' are two songs where their quality stands out by comparison, while 'Strangest Friends' reworks the Crowded House hidden track on 'Nonsense Of Course' from the *Intriguer* sessions.

Out Of The Silence – Neil Finn (2017)
This was a unique musical project in that it was recorded during a global livestream event. With Finn seated at the piano surrounded by his two sons, a string ensemble and a choir of backing singers, these ten songs went out over the world wide web without any editing and were officially released as an album a week later.

Finn's vocal performance throughout is subdued and sincere, as none of these songs require the use of his rockier voice. 'More Than One Of You' and 'Chameleon Days' are highlights, along with the very Crowded House-y 'Second Nature'.

Lightsleeper – Neil and Liam Finn (2018)
With two songs solely attributed to Neil, one credited to all four Finns and the rest a collaboration with Liam, this is a Finn family project like no other. Sadly, the quality of songwriting is disappointing and most of the album, like *Dizzy Heights*, is overproduced and inconsistent. The first three songs are too densely arranged and the vocals are mixed so low that the lyrics are barely distinguishable. 'Anger Plays A Part' and 'Listen' anchor the album's centre as a more listenable section before proceeding towards the end with a fun-with-reverb attitude. Having said this, the partnership between father and son does foretell a sound that emerges on *Dreamers Are Waiting*.

'Find Your Way Back Home' – Single By Neil Finn (2020)
Written and released in benefit of a new housing initiative by the Auckland City Mission, this single features Finn's Fleetwood Mac buddies Stevie Nicks, Christine McVie and Mike Campbell, as well as son Elroy on drums. The slow groove falls in that Neil Finn sweet spot that blends a narrative of despair with a hopeful melody.

Artist In Residence – Todd Rundgren and Neil Finn (2022)
A one-off with the prolific American artist on his album of collaborations,

Space Force. Finn handles most of the vocals in this poppy number, which is reminiscent of 'Deeper Down' from *Dreamers Are Waiting* but with a denser, Rundgren-esque production.

Crowded House Artwork

Besides Neil Finn's craftsmanship as a songwriter and the musicians who have played in the band, there is one more distinguishing factor in making Crowded House unique: Nick Seymour's artwork.

Every Crowded House studio album cover has been an original work of art designed by bassist Seymour, including many of the drawings and images used inside the covers. Moreover, his sense of colour and design has been instrumental in fashioning the stage sets and clothing worn by the band on concert tours and in videos.

Seymour's vivid imagination and playful images helped spark international interest in the band because the visual representation blended so seamlessly with the humour and musical adventurousness of the musicians themselves. That these visuals came directly from inside the band added to their authenticity. Surely, Seymour's paintings came out of the music, just as some of Finn's songs came from visual stimuli. Art inspires art.

Finn reflected on Seymour's designs and process during the 2023 Zoom conversation:

> I have strong memories of him working on covers as we were working on the records. *Temple Of Low Men,* in particular. I've got a video of him putting it together and he's got the soundtrack going. He takes a long time to get around to what he's actually going to do. It's always down to the wire and he feels the pressure of it. So, in his own way, he's doing what I do. Making something up is a bit of a puzzle in his brain.
>
> He's always nervous about bringing his designs to the band. We make a few suggestions here and there. If you put all the records together, they have a continuity which I think is nice. It's like someone's voice that pops through the noise and is identifiable. That individuality goes a long way.

While many musicians have designed artwork for their albums – notably Joni Mitchell, Cat Stevens, Sam Beam (Iron & Wine) and both Lennon and McCartney – it is rare indeed for one band member to have had such complete influence over the art and design of a major musical artist. Seymour's input contributes nearly as much to the Crowded House legacy as the music does.

Although Seymour didn't design the artwork for all Crowded House singles and EP releases, many of his images were used in different contexts. He also had input on the covers for *Farewell To The World* (the live recording from the Sydney Opera House forecourt) released in 2006 and the 2010 compilation *The Very Very Best Of Crowded House*, both of which were designed by long-time collaborator Sharon Chai.

All quotes are taken from interviews with Jeremy Ansell for the Deluxe Edition releases.

Crowded House

Seymour:

> I wanted to do a composite that was similar to the New York artist Sue Coe, who was quite popular at the time with political comic book-type paintings. It was a way of capturing something about each personality. I put Paul in pyjamas because one of his favourite things to do was be around the house in pyjamas preparing for bed, hoping that he would dream and astral travel. And in a way, he felt like an angel in the band. There was something very flighty about his creativity.

The collage-painting features photos of the band members that Seymour has painted over. Seymour himself on the bottom left on a kind of stage, Finn on the bottom right in a red suit with the lyrics to 'Don't Dream It's Over' painted in gold on his jacket, and a winged, bare-chested Hester floating above them on a cushion of air supplied by an electric fan. The curtain that drapes over their stage is decorated with the pyramid and Eye of Providence design seen on the US one-dollar bill.

Seymour:

> There are references to different men's organisations … masonic symbols. Also, the idea of religion with Paul's angelic presence. Nothing specifically anticipates the idea of Paul actually becoming an angel in my lifetime at all. I thought we were going to age gracefully together.

Across the top, there is a classic-looking banner hanging with the name of the band emblazoned across it. The cover is bursting with primary colours and dancing shapes. It's an image that was translated into the visual aesthetic in the first few videos, especially 'World Where You Live'. Also included in that imagery is an erupting volcano featured inside the booklet.

Temple Of Low Men

Another red curtain marks the proscenium of the stage represented on this album cover. This time, Seymour has painted full portraits of himself and his bandmates positioned as they were on the first album: Seymour on the bottom left wearing a jacket festooned with blocks of urban buildings, Finn on the bottom right in a grass-green countryside jacket (including a caravan in the hills) and Hester hanging upside-down in between them with a red velvet jacket to match the curtain.

Regarding Hester being upside-down, Seymour said:

> I wanted to capture Paul's definite mood-swinging or dichotomy of character – I often thought he had schizophrenic moments. I didn't want to play up the clownlike, upside-down fella, court jester idea too much 'cause he didn't

like that. But both times, he actually quite liked the way I painted him or saw him as a member of the group.

Woodface

A wooden mask, its orange and brown tones awash with lines of wood grain and boards askew, adorns the cover. Through the mask's eye, nose and mouth holes, the blackness of the universe is visible, peppered with stars and a distant galaxy. While the name of the band is splashed across the top in lettering that looks like handmade toys, the name of the album doesn't actually appear. The image of the wooden face speaks for itself.

The inside cover features the four faces of the band members surrounded by sawdust. Wood. Face. Get it?

> Finn: My memory is that you brought around ten or 12 images, at least, that you had worked on separately. And you were saying, 'I'm trying to work these all in together as a composite cover.' We saw the wood face image and said, 'Just use that, it's great.'
>
> Seymour: And I actually don't remember how I arrived at the design of a constructed face ... It became an iconic, simple brand that was so simple and obvious. I was delighted that we could go with that.

Together Alone

The cover is an image of a sculpture Seymour fashioned featuring Jesus driving a car with Buddha and Muhammad, the latter discretely hidden behind a curtain with Māori artwork on it. The religious figures are contemporised as they share a ride in a classic red car with fuzzy dice hanging from the rear-view mirror. Nevertheless, there is enough gold leafing around the cover to extol the spiritual virtues of these godly men.

Seymour:

> The cover itself came from conversations we'd had about religions, faith and science. I had decided to try to define the temperament of this discourse in the studio by having prophets all crammed together in this car. I made the mistake of painting a likeness of Muhammad in the back seat.

Richard Thompson, a friend of the band and devout Muslim, upon hearing of the inclusion of Muhammad's image on their album cover, suggested that unless they wanted to face a fatwa against them, they should reconsider.

Seymour:

> I mitigated it with other elements of design. The curtain with the Māori design denoted the nature of Karekare and a lot of the sense of legend that's there.

The name of the band across the top has been carved out of nacre (mother of pearl).

'Recurring Dream'

Darker than other album covers to date, Seymour's painting goes beyond the dreamlike into nightmare territory. Unanswered questions seem to decorate the image that also features references to previous covers: the electric fan from *Crowded House*, the red car from *Together Alone* (and the back cover of *Temple Of Low Men*) and an allusion to the orange woodgrain of *Woodface* in the top corner of the band's name.

The shirtless figure in the car could be a self-portrait and, with its shirt wafting in the wind behind him, is reminiscent of Hester's angel wings on the first album. The top right corner features a curious ear-shaped drawing riddled with numbers and mysterious symbols. For an artist keen on representative art, this cover holds many puzzles.

Afterglow

This cover features busy hands, one pair lighting a cigarette, at a recording studio soundboard overlooking a vista of tall buildings revealed by, once again, red velvet curtains. Extra-large sunglasses rest atop the mixing board, peering out onto green grass and unnaturally blue sky with childlike clouds.

On an album of outtakes and B-sides, this composite image feels appropriately alluring. Neither the band name nor the album title appear anywhere on the original cover.

Seymour:

> It's a combination, again from my journal, of an image I had of the brownstone tenement buildings in Brooklyn. And then a studio control room drawing. The hands were an image I did in the studio of falling down some stairs. It wasn't with anything particularly in mind. It's just ideas thrown together with a deadline.

Time On Earth

Whereas the majority of Crowded House covers cater to the playful, colourful and sometimes cocky side of the band, this one is a direct response to the emotional conditions under which the music was recorded. A lone figure is trapped in the jaws of a serpent as it prowls city streets, with a single tree offering any promise of hope.

The collage is composed entirely of newspaper clippings that Seymour has cut around and painted over. His hand-drawn lettering is graffiti-like over the grey buildings. Only the blue serpent and green treetop provide colour to the otherwise monochromatic artwork.

Seymour:

> That was a graphic image based around the pursuit of an individual living in the urban environment, becoming confined by the space they were living in, unable to leave the house. Once getting out of the house, they are pursued by a monster, like the mythical sea serpent that sailors used to get stir-crazy about. The newspaper reference to these buildings was a narrative of the outside world coming in and creating paranoia. There's a reference to Giotto there and the Tree of Life as well. These are metaphors to describe the thoughts of living in isolation and being prone to mood swings and the like – mental health issues. It was spawned by my concern for Paul.

Intriguer

Seymour:

> I tried so many ways of showing graffiti and the degenerate street art that was in the neighbourhood that Neil's studio is in. I wanted to show something that was quite childlike and benevolent as this child's night light that we had on our mixing desk while we were recording and render that with the menace and integrity of passers-by having turned it into something else. Hence, the inscribing of the word 'Intriguer' reveals the builder's plywood underneath it. And then the sap of the wood coming from where the buttons had been placed in the lettering.

The graffiti motif continues throughout the album layout in Seymour's manipulation of the band photos and Sharon Chai's lyric pages.

Dreamers Are Waiting

Those Crowded House fans who'd dreamed of more music from their favourite band were rewarded with this album cover, a celebration that the long wait was at last over.

A couple of kissing bunnies at the entrance to a cave appear to be the only inhabitants of an island community ('It's just the right size'). As a ruined civilisation overlooks the cobalt sea, symbols of a renaissance represent a hopeful future: a lone shrub growing out of the sand and the rabbits who are known for their ability to reproduce. The viewer is stepping through the grey stones, out of the cave, into a colourful landscape illuminated by a distant sun. All of this is under the title of the album, written in a golden script like something from the Dead Sea Scrolls.

The back cover has two important features: a lamb, which, for centuries, has represented both purity and strength. In the context of *Dreamers Are Waiting*, sheep have long been raised for their meat and their wool, offering warmth and sustenance, which maintains the theme of renaissance. Secondly, a volcano erupts over the horizon line – as one did on *Crowded House* – signifying the continuation of a project that began some 35 years earlier, 'burning and exploding like a slow volcano'.

Gravity Stairs

Seymour creates his best Beatles *Revolver* tribute art as the faces of the musicians – gracing a Crowded House cover for the first time since *Temple Of Low Men* – are etched in black ink on a white background. Each band member has his own unique feature: Neil's hair is coifed with tumultuous waves like one of Hokusai's paintings; Liam's profile, bedecked in swirls and geometric angles, would have fit nicely into the *Temple Of Low Men* motif; Elroy looks off into the distance as a waterfall flows over the left side of his head; Mitchell has a portal carved into his forehead in which sits one of those waving Chinese cat figurines; and Nick himself looks straight ahead, conspicuously devoid of any embellishment.

Squeezed into the negative space above the faces is the simple line graphic with the album title (or, as one television interviewer put it, 'Gravity Stars', as the 'I' in 'STAIRS' seemed to disappear from his view, it being the continuation of the large 'A' in 'GRAVITY' above it). The overwhelmingly monochromatic nature of the cover sets it apart from all other Seymour covers that are rich in colour and texture.

Bonus Question

At the end of the 2023 Zoom conversation, I put Neil Finn on the spot by asking him to name his top five Crowded House songs. As many musicians before him have confessed, it's like trying to choose your favourite child: it's an unfair question and an impossible task. Nevertheless, he was up for it and gamely named five songs that stood out, on that day at least.

> It depends on what day you're asking me really. But I would have to put 'Fall At Your Feet' in there. I'd put 'Don't Dream It's Over' in there because it's had such a huge life. 'Private Universe' – not the record but the song. There are a couple of songs on the new album; I can't really put them in there because you haven't heard them, but … ah, it's really hard. It's such a tough question. I did actually make a big thing about never picking favourites before but here I am trying. 'Say That Again', which you mentioned, I'll just put that in there for a laugh. And there's one on the new album called 'Magic Piano'; I'll put that in there. I don't know; it's really random at this point.

On Track Series

AC/DC – Chris Sutton 978-1-78952-307-2

Allman Brothers Band – Andrew Wild 978-1-78952-252-5

Tori Amos – Lisa Torem 978-1-78952-142-9

Aphex Twin – Beau Waddell 978-1-78952-267-9

Asia – Peter Braidis 978-1-78952-099-6

Badfinger – Robert Day-Webb 978-1-878952-176-4

Barclay James Harvest – Keith and Monica Domone 978-1-78952-067-5

Beck – Arthur Lizie 978-1-78952-258-7

The Beat, General Public, Fine Young Cannibals –
Steve Parry 978-1-78952-274-7

The Beatles – Andrew Wild 978-1-78952-009-5

The Beatles Solo 1969-1980 – Andrew Wild 978-1-78952-030-9

Blue Oyster Cult – Jacob Holm-Lupo 978-1-78952-007-1

Blur – Matt Bishop 978-178952-164-1

Marc Bolan and T.Rex – Peter Gallagher 978-1-78952-124-5

Kate Bush – Bill Thomas 978-1-78952-097-2

The Byrds – Andy McArthur 978-1-78952-280-8

Camel – Hamish Kuzminski 978-1-78952-040-8

Captain Beefheart – Opher Goodwin 978-1-78952-235-8

Caravan – Andy Boot 978-1-78952-127-6

Cardiacs – Eric Benac 978-1-78952-131-3

Wendy Carlos – Mark Marrington 978-1-78952-331-7

The Carpenters – Paul Tornbohm 978-1-78952-301-0

Nick Cave and The Bad Seeds – Dominic Sanderson 978-1-78952-240-2

Eric Clapton Solo – Andrew Wild 978-1-78952-141-2

The Clash – Nick Assirati 978-1-78952-077-4

Elvis Costello and The Attractions – Georg Purvis 978-1-78952-129-0

Crosby, Stills and Nash – Andrew Wild 978-1-78952-039-2

Creedence Clearwater Revival – Tony Thompson 978-178952-237-2

The Damned – Morgan Brown 978-1-78952-136-8

David Bowie 1964 to 1982 – Carl Ewens 978-1-78952-324-9

Deep Purple and Rainbow 1968-79 – Steve Pilkington 978-1-78952-002-6

Depeche Mode – Brian J. Robb 978-1-78952-277-8

Dire Straits – Andrew Wild 978-1-78952-044-6

The Divine Comedy – Alan Draper 978-1-78952-308-9

The Doors – Tony Thompson 978-1-78952-137-5

Dream Theater – Jordan Blum 978-1-78952-050-7

Bob Dylan 1962-1970 – Opher Goodwin 978-1-78952-275-2

Eagles – John Van der Kiste 978-1-78952-260-0

Earth, Wind and Fire – Bud Wilkins 978-1-78952-272-3

Electric Light Orchestra – Barry Delve 978-1-78952-152-8

Emerson Lake and Palmer – Mike Goode 978-1-78952-000-2

Fairport Convention – Kevan Furbank 978-1-78952-051-4

Peter Gabriel – Graeme Scarfe 978-1-78952-138-2

Genesis – Stuart MacFarlane 978-1-78952-005-7

Gentle Giant – Gary Steel 978-1-78952-058-3

Gong – Kevan Furbank 978-1-78952-082-8

Green Day – William E. Spevack 978-1-78952-261-7

Steve Hackett – Geoffrey Feakes 978-1-78952-098-9

Hall and Oates – Ian Abrahams 978-1-78952-167-2

Peter Hammill – Richard Rees Jones 978-1-78952-163-4

Roy Harper – Opher Goodwin 978-1-78952-130-6

Hawkwind (new edition) – Duncan Harris 978-1-78952-290-7

Jimi Hendrix – Emma Stott 978-1-78952-175-7

The Hollies – Andrew Darlington 978-1-78952-159-7

Horslips – Richard James 978-1-78952-263-1

The Human League and The Sheffield Scene – Andrew Darlington 978-1-78952-186-3

Humble Pie –Robert Day-Webb 978-1-78952-2761

Ian Hunter – G. Mick Smith 978-1-78952-304-1

The Incredible String Band – Tim Moon 978-1-78952-107-8

INXS – Manny Grillo 978-1-78952-302-7

Iron Maiden – Steve Pilkington 978-1-78952-061-3

Joe Jackson – Richard James 978-1-78952-189-4

The Jam – Stan Jeffries 978-1-78952-299-0

Jefferson Airplane – Richard Butterworth 978-1-78952-143-6

Jethro Tull – Jordan Blum 978-1-78952-016-3

Elton John in the 1970s – Peter Kearns 978-1-78952-034-7

Billy Joel – Lisa Torem 978-1-78952-183-2

Judas Priest – John Tucker 978-1-78952-018-7

Kansas – Kevin Cummings 978-1-78952-057-6

Killing Joke – Nic Ransome 978-1-78952-273-0

The Kinks – Martin Hutchinson 978-1-78952-172-6

Korn – Matt Karpe 978-1-78952-153-5

Led Zeppelin – Steve Pilkington 978-1-78952-151-1

Level 42 – Matt Philips 978-1-78952-102-3

Little Feat – Georg Purvis – 978-1-78952-168-9

Magnum – Matthew Taylor – 978-1-78952-286-0

Aimee Mann – Jez Rowden 978-1-78952-036-1

Ralph McTell – Paul O. Jenkins 978-1-78952-294-5

Metallica – Barry Wood 978-1-78952-269-3

Joni Mitchell – Peter Kearns 978-1-78952-081-1

The Moody Blues – Geoffrey Feakes 978-1-78952-042-2

Motorhead – Duncan Harris 978-1-78952-173-3

Nektar – Scott Meze – 978-1-78952-257-0

New Order – Dennis Remmer – 978-1-78952-249-5

Nightwish – Simon McMurdo – 978-1-78952-270-9

Nirvana – William E. Spevack 978-1-78952-318-8

Laura Nyro – Philip Ward 978-1-78952-182-5

Oasis – 978-1-78952-300-3

Mike Oldfield – Ryan Yard 978-1-78952-060-6

Opeth – Jordan Blum 978-1-78-952-166-5

Pearl Jam – Ben L. Connor 978-1-78952-188-7

Tom Petty – Richard James 978-1-78952-128-3

Pink Floyd – Richard Butterworth 978-1-78952-242-6

The Police – Pete Braidis 978-1-78952-158-0

Porcupine Tree – Nick Holmes 978-1-78952-144-3

Procol Harum – Scott Meze 978-1-78952-315-7

Queen – Andrew Wild 978-1-78952-003-3

Radiohead – William Allen 978-1-78952-149-8

Rancid – Paul Matts 978-1-78952-187-0

Lou Reed 1972-1986 – Ethan Roy 978-1-78952-283-9

Renaissance – David Detmer 978-1-78952-062-0

REO Speedwagon – Jim Romag 978-1-78952-262-4

The Rolling Stones 1963-80 – Steve Pilkington 978-1-78952-017-0

Linda Ronstadt 1969-1989 – Daryl O. Lawrence 987-1-78952-293-8

Sensational Alex Harvey Band – Peter Gallagher 978-1-7952-289-1

The Small Faces and The Faces – Andrew Darlington 978-1-78952-316-4

The Smashing Pumpkins – Matt Karpe 978-1-7952-291-4

The Smiths and Morrissey – Tommy Gunnarsson 978-1-78952-140-5

Spirit – Rev. Keith A. Gordon – 978-1-78952- 248-8

Soft Machine – Scott Meze 978-1078952-271-6

Stackridge – Alan Draper 978-1-78952-232-7

Status Quo the Frantic Four Years – Richard James 978-1-78952-160-3

Steely Dan – Jez Rowden 978-1-78952-043-9

The Stranglers – Martin Hutchinson 978-1-78952-323-2

Talk Talk – Gary Steel 978-1-78952-284-6

Tears For Fears – Paul Clark – 978-178952-238-9

Thin Lizzy – Graeme Stroud 978-1-78952-064-4

Tool – Matt Karpe 978-1-78952-234-1

Toto – Jacob Holm-Lupo 978-1-78952-019-4

U2 – Eoghan Lyng 978-1-78952-078-1

UFO – Richard James 978-1-78952-073-6

Ultravox – Brian J. Robb 978-1-78952-330-0

Van Der Graaf Generator – Dan Coffey 978-1-78952-031-6

Van Halen – Morgan Brown – 9781-78952-256-3

Suzanne Vega – Lisa Torem 978-1-78952-281-5

Jack White And The White Stripes – Ben L. Connor 978-1-78952-303-4

The Who – Geoffrey Feakes 978-1-78952-076-7

Roy Wood and the Move – James R Turner 978-1-78952-008-8

Yes (new edition) – Stephen Lambe 978-1-78952-282-2

Neil Young 1963 to 1970 – Oper Goodwin 978-1-78952-298-3

Frank Zappa 1966 to 1979 – Eric Benac 978-1-78952-033-0

Warren Zevon – Peter Gallagher 978-1-78952-170-2

The Zombies – Emma Stott 978-1-78952-297-6

10CC – Peter Kearns 978-1-78952-054-5

Decades Series

The Bee Gees in the 1960s – Andrew Mon Hughes et al 978-1-78952-148-1
The Bee Gees in the 1970s – Andrew Mon Hughes et al 978-1-78952-179-5
Black Sabbath in the 1970s – Chris Sutton 978-1-78952-171-9
Britpop – Peter Richard Adams and Matt Pooler 978-1-78952-169-6
Phil Collins in the 1980s – Andrew Wild 978-1-78952-185-6
Alice Cooper in the 1970s – Chris Sutton 978-1-78952-104-7
Alice Cooper in the 1980s – Chris Sutton 978-1-78952-259-4
Curved Air in the 1970s – Laura Shenton 978-1-78952-069-9
Donovan in the 1960s – Jeff Fitzgerald 978-1-78952-233-4
Bob Dylan in the 1980s – Don Klees 978-1-78952-157-3
Brian Eno in the 1970s – Gary Parsons 978-1-78952-239-6
Faith No More in the 1990s – Matt Karpe 978-1-78952-250-1
Fleetwood Mac in the 1970s – Andrew Wild 978-1-78952-105-4
Fleetwood Mac in the 1980s – Don Klees 978-178952-254-9
Focus in the 1970s – Stephen Lambe 978-1-78952-079-8
Free and Bad Company in the 1970s – John Van der Kiste 978-1-78952-178-8
Genesis in the 1970s – Bill Thomas 978178952-146-7
George Harrison in the 1970s – Eoghan Lyng 978-1-78952-174-0
Kiss in the 1970s – Peter Gallagher 978-1-78952-246-4
Manfred Mann's Earth Band in the 1970s –
John Van der Kiste 978178952-243-3
Marillion in the 1980s – Nathaniel Webb 978-1-78952-065-1
Van Morrison in the 1970s – Peter Childs – 978-1-78952-241-9
Mott the Hoople & Ian Hunter in the 1970s –
John Van der Kiste 978-1-78-952-162-7
Pink Floyd In The 1970s – Georg Purvis 978-1-78952-072-9
Suzi Quatro in the 1970s – Darren Johnson 978-1-78952-236-5
Queen in the 1970s – James Griffiths 978-1-78952-265-5
Roxy Music in the 1970s – Dave Thompson 978-1-78952-180-1
Slade in the 1970s – Darren Johnson 978-1-78952-268-6
Status Quo in the 1980s – Greg Harper 978-1-78952-244-0
Tangerine Dream in the 1970s – Stephen Palmer 978-1-78952-161-0
The Sweet in the 1970s – Darren Johnson 978-1-78952-139-9
Uriah Heep in the 1970s – Steve Pilkington 978-1-78952-103-0

Van der Graaf Generator in the 1970s – Steve Pilkington 978-1-78952-245-7

Rick Wakeman in the 1970s – Geoffrey Feakes 978-1-78952-264-8

Yes in the 1980s – Stephen Lambe with David Watkinson 978-1-78952-125-2

Rock Classics Series

90125 by Yes – Stephen Lambe 978-1-78952-329-4

Bat Out Of Hell by Meatloaf – Geoffrey Feakes 978-1-78952-320-1

Bringing It All Back Home by Bob Dylan – Opher Goodwin 978-1-78952-314-0

Crime Of The Century by Supertramp – Steve Pilkington 978-1-78952-327-0

Let It Bleed by The Rolling Stones – John Van der Kiste 978-1-78952-309-6

Purple Rain by Prince – Matt Karpe 978-1-78952-322-5

On Screen Series

Carry On… – Stephen Lambe 978-1-78952-004-0

David Cronenberg – Patrick Chapman 978-1-78952-071-2

Doctor Who: The David Tennant Years – Jamie Hailstone 978-1-78952-066-8

James Bond – Andrew Wild 978-1-78952-010-1

Monty Python – Steve Pilkington 978-1-78952-047-7

Seinfeld Seasons 1 to 5 – Stephen Lambe 978-1-78952-012-5

Other Books

1967: A Year In Psychedelic Rock 978-1-78952-155-9

1970: A Year In Rock – John Van der Kiste 978-1-78952-147-4

1972: The Year Progressive Rock Ruled The World – Kevan Furbank 978-1-78952-288-4

1973: The Golden Year of Progressive Rock 978-1-78952-165-8

Babysitting A Band On The Rocks – G.D. Praetorius 978-1-78952-106-1

Eric Clapton Sessions – Andrew Wild 978-1-78952-177-1

Dark Horse Records – Aaron Badgley 978-1-78952-287-7

Derek Taylor: For Your Radioactive Children – Andrew Darlington 978-1-78952-038-5

The Golden Age of Easy Listening – Derek Taylor 978-1-78952-285-3

The Golden Road: The Recording History of The Grateful Dead – John Kilbride 978-1-78952-156-6

Iggy and The Stooges On Stage 1967-1974 – Per Nilsen 978-1-78952-101-6

Jon Anderson and the Warriors – the road to Yes –
David Watkinson 978-1-78952-059-0

Magic: The David Paton Story – David Paton 978-1-78952-266-2

Misty: The Music of Johnny Mathis – Jakob Baekgaard 978-1-78952-247-1

Nu Metal: A Definitive Guide – Matt Karpe 978-1-78952-063-7

Remembering Live Aid – Andrew Wild 978-1-78952-328-7

Tommy Bolin: In and Out of Deep Purple – Laura Shenton 978-1-78952-070-5

Maximum Darkness – Deke Leonard 978-1-78952-048-4

The Twang Dynasty – Deke Leonard 978-1-78952-049-1

And Many More To Come!

Would you like to write for Sonicbond Publishing?

At Sonicbond Publishing we are always on the look-out for authors, particularly for our two main series:

On Track. Mixing fact with in depth analysis, the On Track series examines the work of a particular musical artist or group. All genres are considered from easy listening and jazz to 60s soul to 90s pop, via rock and metal.

On Screen. This series looks at the world of film and television. Subjects considered include directors, actors and writers, as well as entire television and film series. As with the On Track series, we balance fact with analysis.

While professional writing experience would, of course, be an advantage the most important qualification is to have real enthusiasm and knowledge of your subject. First-time authors are welcomed, but the ability to write well in English is essential.

Sonicbond Publishing has distribution throughout Europe and North America, and all books are also published in E-book form. Authors will be paid a royalty based on sales of their book.

Further details are available from www.sonicbondpublishing.co.uk. To contact us, complete the contact form there or email info@sonicbondpublishing.co.uk